Bishop of Southwell

Period of My Life

by
F. R. BARRY

Sometime Bishop of Southwell

HODDER AND STOUGHTON
LONDON · SYDNEY · AUCKLAND · TORONTO

For Lilian,
in gratitude

Contents

Illustrations

Acknowledgements

I OFFER grateful acknowledgements to the Cork Historical and Archaeological Society for permission to reproduce information from its *Journal* in Chapter I; to Victor Gollancz Ltd. for the extract from Dr. James Parkes' *Voyage of Discoveries* on page 91 and Messrs. Hutchinson for the quotations from Mayhew's *Party Games* on the same page; to Canon Jasper, the Oxford University Press and the *Daily Telegraph* for the quotation from Liddell Hart on page 152; and to the Proprietors of *Punch* for permission to reprint the lines on page 131. The photograph of Archbishop Davidson at Le Touquet was kindly lent me by the Rev. E. R. Wildbore, who had somehow preserved it, and my brother Harold took the snapshot of Manorbier for me.

If I have unwittingly infringed any copyrights, I make due apologies.

Preface

THIS IS SOMETHING that I had never meant to do and indeed
have often insisted that I would not do. I can devour any
autobiography, for it fascinates me to learn what other people
have seen in their journey through this ambiguous world; but I
never intended to write one myself. I could not suppose that my
life had been so important that anybody would want to read a
book about it. Yet here am I trying to do this very thing. My
resolution was rather undermined by the reception given to a
previous book. Ever since the publication of *Mervyn Haigh* I
have been under strong and constant pressure, both from my
family and close friends and from high ecclesiastical authority,
to put together some memoirs on my own account. It was urged
that, as I had lived through a past which to the young is now
prehistoric, they might have some useful light to throw on that.
It was even suggested that there would be a welcome for them.
I kept these blandishments at arm's length because there was
still other writing to get finished. But when I had almost 'come
to four-score years' it was clear that if this job was to be done at
all, it could not be delayed any longer. So I set to work, and
here is the result.

What I wanted to write — and this was the only way in
which in my view such a venture could be justified or have any
interest for anyone else — was a kind of autobiographical
commentary on the period covered by my generation, and so,
through the life and experience of one man, to illustrate some
aspects of the movement from the pre-war to the post-war
situation. But here I have laboured under a disadvantage. For

it so happens that, owing to the air-raids and the total destruction of all my books and records, I do not possess one scrap of paper prior to May 1941; and even such notes as I brought away from Southwell managed to get mislaid during the move and only reappeared when the book was finished. Consequently I have had to rely almost exclusively on my unaided memory — though my wife has been able to check some of the dates for me. And 'old men forget'. More than once I have had to leave out some incident through inability to recall a name! But all this means that what the reader will find here is not so much an entirely objective narrative of events 'as they actually happened', as the deposit left in my own mind — the thoughts and experiences of a younger man as now seen in the memory of an older man, and therefore to some extent editorialised. And no doubt I have therefore sometimes put a more favourable construction on my own actions than others may have put on them at the time.

There is at present an awful amount of talk both about Christianity itself and about the future of the Church, but too little evidence of thought in depth. 'Progressivism' may be as superficial in the field of religion as it can be in politics. The *avant garde* are impatient of tradition and seem to assume that whatever is traditional must, simply for that reason, be wrong. But the Christian faith is anchored in a tradition, handed down through the generations. If there is no conservation of tradition, if accumulated human experience is not transmitted from one age to the next and each new generation must start again from scratch, how much real advance will be possible? There is no way forward by ignoring history. I offer here just a footnote to one chapter in the long story of the Church of England.

Several friends kindly read the first draft and have helped me much by their advice and criticism. Perhaps I should point out that the completed typescript left my hands at the end of February. In what follows, accordingly, there is no mention of anything that has happened since then. A few sentences are out of date already. But I leave the text without any alteration, except that, for reasons which are explained there, I have added a postscript to it in proof.

Westminster   F. R. B.
  July 1970

I

Home Background

BY BIRTH AND upbringing I am a late Victorian. When I was born in 1890 Archbishop Benson reigned at Lambeth and the 'great' Lord Salisbury was Prime Minister, between two of Mr. Gladstone's administrations. In my journey through life I have travelled a long way from that settled world of unquestioning conformity to this age of revolution and insecurity in which all traditions are being called in question and pre-war means benighted or morally wrong. I have had to keep on learning all the time, and often, it seems, to be starting all over again. Each of the wars has meant a radical break. Theological thought has moved into a world in which now, in old age, I have had to attempt to learn a new alphabet and a new grammar. Yet a life, like history, is continuous; and the only justification of these memoirs must be that mine happens to have synchronised with a critical and formative period in our social and religious development about which the younger generation know little.

It has been my privilege to enjoy the friendship of some of the leading figures who played their part in it, and some of the posts I have held have allowed me to see a good many different aspects of Church life, both in this country and overseas. At the end of my time perhaps I was myself fairly well known in the Church of England. But the Church itself has been changing all through these years, and it is today a society very different from that in which our generation grew up; indeed I sometimes feel that most of the things I cared for and worked for are being swept away. Maybe something better will take their place. But in any case, I am now on the way out, and though few will want to read anything about me, some may care to know something about the period as reflected in one man's experience. My title, therefore, is my excuse for writing.

My father's family was Norman-Irish, and we have behind us a very ancient lineage, which can be traced back to the eleventh century. Barry, like Montgomery, is a Norman name which appears in the roll of Battle Abbey. This may now be regarded as rather shaky evidence, but a Barry is found securely in history from at least the beginning of the twelfth century —not however, in England, but in Wales. When the Normans overran the Welsh coastlands they established their followers as marcher lords; and one, the first identified Barry, was given the tenure of Barry (St. Barroch's) island, from which he took the name of de Barri and built Barry Castle on the mainland. His son (or grandson?), William de Barri, who is described as Baron of Pembroke (born 1110), had his seat at Manorbier (Maynaupir) Castle in Pembrokeshire, which we regard as the ancestral home. He married Hangaret, daughter of Gerald de Windsor (whose father was constable of Windsor Castle) by his wife Nesta, who was herself the daughter of Rhys ap Tudor, Prince of South Wales. By this marriage there were four sons, Philip (the ancestor of our line), Robert, Edward and Gerald. This youngest son, Gerald Fitzstephen de Barri, Archdeacon of Brecknock, is the distinguished personage known to historians as Giraldus Cambrensis ('three-quarters Norman, a quarter Welsh') who wrote such a loving appreciation of Manorbier, and from whom this account of our origins is derived.[1] William was succeeded by the eldest son, Philip, who resided at Manorbier Castle and was buried in the adjoining parish church. Yet from now on the scene shifts to Ireland, where again the Norman nobility were employed to effect and hold down the

[1] All the information reproduced in this section I owe to a series of long, learned and detailed articles based on extant genealogies by the late Rev. Edmond Barry in the *Journal of the Cork Historical and Archaeological Society* beginning January, 1899. I am grateful for permission to use it.

16

conquest. William de Barri's brother-in-law, Robert Fitz-stephen, was one of the commanders in the expedition, and after it Henry II invested him with land amounting to half the kingdom of Cork. From this estate he made over three baronies to his nephew Philip, who had taken part in the invasion, including the lordships of Olethan and Barrymore, which remained in the family for centuries. This was how the Barrys came to be Irish.

For they quickly rooted themselves in southern Ireland and fanned out in an intricate pattern of branches, with halls (or castles) in various parts of Munster. Some 'became mere Irish Chieftains, many assuming Irish names and being entirely hostile to the English government' (Wagner, *English Genealogy* (OUP, 1960) p. 75). The family held the Viscounty of Butte-vant[2] – in 1490 William Barry was summoned to Parliament at Westminster as the premier viscount of Ireland – which was later merged in the earldom of Barrymore, conferred by Charles I on David Fitzgerald who, having first sided with the rebels, then changed sides and fought against Desmond. (The earldom became extinct in 1823.) These were savage times and some of these were rough men, engaged either in fighting and buc-caneering or in killing off Barry claimants to their own titles. But there is in existence a pedigree, given to Sir George Carew by David, Viscount Buttevant, which traces direct descent from Philip to himself in 1602. Thence it runs (though here the tree is complicated) to the Barrys of Dundellerick, from whom it descends directly to my grandfather. Like the Vikings turned farmers in our Lakeland valleys, by the seventeenth century they had settled down into bourgeois respectability – some doctors, some parsons, most of them just plain 'gent'.

The most colourful exhibit of these later times (though it dates in fact from the nineteenth century) was Dr. James Barry (1795–1865), 'the most skilful of physicians, the most wayward of men', who served as an army doctor (and fought a duel) at the Cape, was threatened more than once with court martial,

[2] Buttevant is Norman for Push ahead – *bouttez en avant*.

rose to the top of the military ladder as Inspector General of Army Medical Services — and was found at death to have been a woman! This feat earned her a place in the *Dictionary of National Biography*.

Edmond Fitzjames Barry of Dundellerick is documented in or about 1660. Sixth from him was David Thomas, my grandfather, in holy orders, who married Anne McKee and had by her three sons — Russell, after whom I was named, David, the 'Uncle X' of an earlier book of mine, and (his youngest child) George Duncan, my father—and two daughters, Mary and Geraldine, the terrifying aunts of our childhood. In early manhood my grandfather left Ireland and held certain preferments in England, one of which was a parish in Birkenhead. He also served for a time as a chaplain in the Indian Ecclesiastical Establishment, and the two elder sons made their career in India, Russell to become in due course a judge, and David an engineer in the Indian Railways. He lived on till 1904, as rector of a mini-parish in Norfolk. But before he went east, his youngest (my father) had been born in 1864 — in Birkenhead — the first of our line to be born in England since the beginning of the twelfth century.

One branch (as I discovered when I went to Southwell) had taken root in Nottinghamshire. According to Domesday Book, Galfridus de Barri (or de insula, i.e. Barry Island) held the Manor of Teversal in that county. Ranulphus (probably his younger son) is recorded in 1140 as Lord of Tollerton and as having given the church to Lenton Priory. These Barrys were Lords of the Manor of Tollerton from then onwards until near the end of the sixteenth century. When John Barry died without issue (1545) his sister succeeded and married Richard Pendock, who became Lord of the Manor in right of his wife. The succession henceforth is through Pendocks, Neales and Otters (names still prominent in that part of the world) who do not really belong to the Barry line. The last appearance of the name was when Robert Melvil Barry Otter Barry assumed the 'Barry' on inheriting the Tollerton estate, which he sold in 1873. It then disappears from Nottinghamshire history.[3]

Of my mother's family I know almost nothing, and there is nobody now alive who does know. Her father had been a naval officer, Commander Reid, R.N. – there were legends about his having captured slave ships. But he died before my birth and I never knew him. Our grandmother, Mrs. Reid, I remember vividly. In the white widow's bonnet of her period, she looked exactly like Queen Victoria – and indeed was, on occasion, mistaken for her and greeted with cheers in public places. (It is hard to believe that Victoria R and I would have gone around on her feet and unattended.) She lived in a house on the sea front in Dover, where we spent the summer holiday, and we would sit hour by hour on her balcony scanning the Channel through binoculars and identifying the ships as they passed.

My father, after he went down from Cambridge, acted as tutor to a young gentleman whom he conducted on a visit to Rome. Mrs. Reid and her daughter had been in Rome at the time, and when he contracted a severe fever, Miss Geraldine Reid devotedly nursed him through it. Their engagement inevitably followed, and they were married in 1888. I was the first child of the marriage. So I am half Irish and half English; and this may perhaps have produced a certain mixture of Irish imagination and Saxon realism. And whenever I have been asked to Ireland, to preach at Trinity or in St. Patrick's, I have always felt that I half-belonged there. These invitations have given immense enjoyment.

The earliest memory that I can recall is that of feeding the pigeons in Rochester Castle. My father was a curate at St. Peter's, newly married, with me their first baby. But I have no further recollection of Rochester, for my parents moved before I was three years old. The next time I saw it was when, as a

[3] I owe these facts to the researches of my former Registrar, Mr. Richard Beaumont, and to Thoroton's *History of Nottinghamshire*, 1, 171.

Fellow of Oriel, I stayed a weekend with G. A. Cooke, then Oriel Professor of Holy Scripture, whose chair was at that time based on a Rochester canonry.

The move was to Surbiton, where my father was to join the staff of St. Mark's, and a little terraced villa in Berrylands Road was to be the background of my small-boy period. Surbiton, then one of the outer suburbs in the stockbroker and executive belt, was still within the Rochester diocese (which included all London south of the Thames) of which Randall Davidson had just become Bishop. Mandell Creighton was consecrated to Peterborough the same day. Many years later I was to be admitted to the confidence of Archbishop Davidson and to have Mrs. Creighton, then residing in Oxford, as a member of my parochial church council. But in early childhood I heard the praises of Davidson. When the child born after me died in infancy, he wrote my father a personal letter of sympathy – a "wonderful thing for a bishop to do" in those days – and my father told people about it again and again. (It would be an odd bishop who failed to do it nowadays.) The parish contained a number of wealthy people and St. Mark's under Archdeacon Burney was what was then known as a fashionable church. It went in for very elaborate musical services: High Mattins and Evensong were 'fully choral' – they even sang the General Confession! –and any chance moment of silence was quickly dispelled by an organ voluntary. Sung Eucharists, of course, were unimaginable; they were the sinister rites of 'extreme ritualists'; and this prejudice of Victorian protestantism took a surprisingly long time to die. Even just before the second war my congregation at St. John's, Westminster, viewed with great suspicion my proposal to introduce a few hymns at Holy Communion. "The next thing will be servers" – a terrible thought. The daughter church, St. Andrew's, was 'high', that is, the clergy wore coloured stoles, which was about halfway to Roman catholicism. There was also, I think, a slum 'district' safely hidden behind the façade.

St. Mark's had a staff of three or four; curates were plentiful and dreadfully cheap—how cheap, we children knew on our pulses. My parents' family grew year by year and ours was a desperately poor home always harassed by pinchbeck economies. We were dressed in the cast-off clothes of wealthy parishioners. We realised this and bitterly resented it. I remember a moment of domestic tragedy. My father somehow lost a gold sovereign—perhaps a week's household expenditure[4] and the family was plunged in distress till some rich men in the congregation did a whip round and gave him a purse containing five new gold pieces. We had never seen anything like it before. Ever since, I have loved the parable about the woman and her lost coin. Jesus knew what it meant in a poor home. It was, I suppose, to eke out his pittance income that my father became an Inspector of church schools, and was often away in south London or elsewhere.

Archdeacon Burney, whose curates were afraid of him and were required to address him as Sir, was venerable not only in title. He was old and tottery with a failing memory—on occasion he left out the Consecration prayer. But at that time the Church had no pension scheme. An incumbent could cripple a parish if he resigned, when he was entitled to take a third of the income. For the Church it was therefore the lesser of two evils that he should hold on till death them should part. (The same applied also, at that time, to bishoprics—till the bishops surrendered their statutory right for a smaller, contributory pension.)

We were a devoted and closely united family, deeply attached to our parents and one another. A new baby arrived almost every twelve months; babies were born in the home in those days, and we learnt to recognise the signs (the sudden arrival of Nurse Dixon) and to make the appropriate responses. But I now scarcely remember my mother at all, for she died in 1898 at the birth of my youngest brother Gerald, having borne six

[4] I don't know exactly what the stipend was, but the curates at Garbett's Portsea, much later, were paid £120 a year, and he took £90 of it for board and lodging. The rest was for clothes, books, holidays and pocketmoney.

children in eight years. (The Church taught then and that generation believed that what we now accept as a Christian duty was contrary to the law of God. I imply no criticism of my father.) My mother's death was a shattering blow to the young family and most of all to our father, left desolate with five small children on his hands. He dramatised his grief, as Victorians did, but for years after he was a stricken man, and though he held on bravely for our sakes he very nearly, I think, lost his reason. They were passionately in love with one another and the spring had gone out of his year. For me it was a deeply traumatic experience, leaving me an unhappy and introverted child who could not easily relate to other children, making me hate school instead of enjoying it. In spite of our happy marriage and so much else I think I have never entirely recovered from being left in childhood without a mother.

When Gerald found out the facts about his birth it induced in him a gnawing guilt-complex by which he was tormented throughout his life. He was far and away the most gifted of us. A dreamy child and a late developer, he showed himself in manhood a genius, with an astonishingly wide range of gifts, executive drive and an irresistible charm. He came into public prominence and a knighthood (and an honorary FRIBA) as Director of the Festival of Britain (nominated by Herbert Morrison, then Home Secretary) and rehabilitator of the South Bank, evincing powers which nobody knew he possessed. He died in 1968, on his seventieth birthday after agonising pain from cancer, which he bore with heroic unselfishness and fortitude. His obituary in *The Times* and the memorial service in St. Paul's bore witness not only to what he had achieved but still more to his own fundamental goodness. In his later years he had moved (or thought he had) some way from traditional Christian belief, and began to describe himself as an agnostic. But I think of him as a grand Christian character and thank God for his inward integrity.

The baby sister who had preceded Gerald died of infantile meningitis very shortly after our mother's death, and my sister

Margot, who was a semi-invalid, died soon after the end of the first war. Thus, of the six only two of us now survive — my eldest sister Dorothy and myself. After a series of governesses and housekeepers, my father subsequently remarried. Our stepmother was Miss Fanny Ekin, a former parishioner of St. Mark, Surbiton, who had idolised him from afar. This brought him deep satisfaction, though she took on a harder job than perhaps she realised; and to her incredible courage and devotion we owe more than can be put into words. There were two sons of the second marriage — Harold, who after having had to come back from educational service in India became an HMI in the north of England and, on compulsory retirement, a research fellow of Manchester University; and Philip, who, after holding various town parishes, is now Rector of Seddlescombe in Sussex.

As children we went to an old-fashioned dame school, where we learnt to read and write and do sums and to memorise the kings and queens of England. It must have been shortly before our mother's death, when I was about seven or eight, that I was sent as a dayboy to Shrewsbury House, a prep school for the Surbiton well-to-do. (No doubt I was taken free or at reduced terms.) Shrewsbury House was probably fairly primitive at that time by modern educational standards, but Woodhouse, the headmaster, was very kind to me and gave me a solid grounding in the classics which got me the scholarship at Bradfield (after a dismal failure at Winchester, due to my ineptitude at mathematics) without which I could never have been educated; I am duly grateful for what I owe to him. I very well remember the Boer War — we collected pipes for the absent-minded beggar — and the jubilations on the relief of Mafeking, and the atmosphere of vulgar, unthinking jingoism which afflicted English society at the time. I have also memories of the Diamond Jubilee and of my father bringing home a copy of the *Daily Mail* printed in gold type. The naval review in that year was the symbol of climactic imperial arrogance and optimism. But Kipling's 'Recessional' sounded the misgiving. Wholly unconscious of it though we were, that world was already beginning to break up. It is easy enough to realise that in retrospect, but none of us could have imagined it at the time; so that when the war came in 1914 it fell like a thunderbolt out of a blue sky on a people totally unprepared to face it.

One scene that remains in memory from childhood is that of the two superb figures of King Edward VII and the Kaiser riding side by side at Queen Victoria's funeral, which I watched from a window in London, though I cannot imagine now how we got the chance.

About two years after my mother's death our family life was dramatically changed. His college (Caius) offered my father a country living. It was not in the least what he would have chosen, and indeed it foreclosed any such 'career' as he may have imagined and probably could have had; for in those days to become a country parson was to rub oneself off the ecclesiastical map — "Abandon hope, all ye who enter here", as the country clergy themselves often quoted. But he accepted it largely for our sakes, as providing a better environment for his children; and that was altogether in character. Only as I grew up did I come to realise at what cost to himself the decision had been made. But to me it brought a lifelong enrichment. I shall always be thankful to have grown to manhood against the background of Norfolk rectories. It gave me a deep and abiding love of the country — I have ever since been a countryman at heart — and some understanding of agricultural processes. I learnt as a boy to drive a plough on the glebe farm. And it gave me later, when I became a bishop, some better insight into the opportunities and the difficulties of the village parishes and the life and ministry of the country clergy.

So we were translated to Long Stratton, a village some ten miles from Norwich, and to what would now be called an 'impossible' rectory in which, till he put one in, there was no bathroom, no piped water (it had to be pumped from a well by heavy labour an hour every morning) and in which all the

windows faced north. There were no diocesan committees then
to look after or modernise the parsonages, no system of payment
for dilapidations. The whole expense of maintenance or
improvement fell on the income of the benefice, which was
perhaps £300 a year. How my father did it and brought up a
family and paid for our education on that income, I cannot
even begin to imagine. It was, of course, a time of cheap prices.
Eggs were sold a twenty for a shilling, coal was nineteen shillings
a ton, an enormous tea in a farmhouse cost sixpence, a gardener's wage was twenty shillings a week.[5] We always seem to
have had domestic servants (wages about £20 a year) a
governess or nanny and a gardener. My father eked out his
stipend by taking pupils – mysterious boys who, as I now suppose, had somehow come to grief at their public schools – and
by examining for the 'Cambridge locals'. But he never had a
penny to spend on himself. He could never, for instance, buy a
book, and he had the tastes and the making of a scholar. (He
took a B.D. at Cambridge in later life.) I am humbled to think
of the sacrifices he made for us.

The fact is that in those days, broadly speaking, a 'living' was
not regarded as a livelihood. Many of the clergy still had private
means, and the living was just a bit of additional pocketmoney.
But those who had to depend altogether on their benefices were
desperately hard-up. One summer at Long Stratton it was
announced that not merely a circus but two circuses were about
to visit the village. I ran into the study in great excitement and
asked if I might be allowed to go to both. I have never forgotten
my father's answer. "You know," he said, "that I will do my
best for you; but I cannot promise to be able to give you sixpence twice in one week." I am grateful for having had to learn
that lesson. It taught me to do without what I could not have,
and it gave me, as bishop, some inside knowledge of what was
really going on in the vicarages.

For us children the move was like a translation to paradise.
We exchanged a backyard for a huge overgrown garden full of

[5] For the other side of that picture see p. 29.

all manner of mysteries and enjoyments, with red squirrels running up and down the trees and a wonderful orchestra of birds. Owls and nightingales kept us awake in bed! There were stables in which we could keep our rabbits. In the way of their kind they were fruitful and multiplied. I once had fifty. (My father very wisely sold them off to the market while I was away at school.) Of course there were no amusements laid on, and we had to devise our own without spending money. When I was at home in the school holidays I spent most of my time with Farmer Dye, the beloved, if feckless tenant of the Glebe farm.

East Anglia was then still a world of its own, with its own dialect, which we delighted to speak, its characteristic customs and traditions, quite unlike any other part of England and indeed something like a distinct nation. Its way of life has been brilliantly recalled by Ronald Blythe in his superb book, *Akenfield* (Penguin Books, 1969). Norfolk was then totally 'unspoiled' and unvisited by any disturbing modernisms. The social structure was unashamedly feudal — the Big House, the Rectory, the tenant farmers, and, far below, the serfs, the cottagers.[6] (This at least was the Victorian order of things. It was only since the eighteenth century, with the rise in the price of corn, that the country clergy had been accepted as gentlemen.) The villages were completely self-contained. We hear now about the loneliness of the clergy, but it is cultural now not geographical. They might have thought themselves lonely in our time, with no telephones and no public transport and, of course, no cars, but they managed to get around, travelling by ponytrap or pushbike, and to meet one another quite often. The 'horseless carriage' was just on the way in. I remember seeing one of the first, at Surbiton, preceded by a man with a red flag. But it had not yet penetrated into the country — and it 'scared the horses', which was unforgivable. My father once bicycled into Norwich at panic speed at two o'clock in the

[6] The situation a generation earlier has been brilliantly recaptured by Dr. Owen Chadwick in his *A Victorian Miniature* (Hodder & Stoughton, 1960).

morning to fetch a surgeon, who came in a horse buggy, to perform an emergency operation. If we had to go to the station (Forncett Junction) we hired the village grocer's cart; two miles each way, and it cost a whole shilling. When the bishop (Sheepshanks) came for a confirmation, he presumably came to Forncett by train; but he would arrive, in top-hat with strings, and gaiters, sitting on the box of a one-horse cab. He would stay the night and go back again the next day. Bishops' lives must have been pretty restful when it took two days to keep a single engagement! But what could they do, with such slow communications? They could not achieve that ubiquity in space which is now thought to inhere in the office of bishop — whether for better or for worse, who knows? A nineteenth-century Primate recorded how much he enjoyed 'sitting quietly at Lambeth'. They certainly did not suffer from overwork!

But it was, I confess, rather a surprise to me to find a modern bishop in that happy state. When I was Vicar of St. Mary's, Oxford, I wrote to my bishop, Tommy Strong, to ask his advice about some problem or other. He told me to go and see him at Cuddesdon. He solved my problem for me in a few minutes and then engaged me in general conversation. Then he kindly invited me to stay for lunch[7] and went on chatting well into the afternoon. At last for very shame I got up and apologised for taking so much of his time. He was the bishop of the largest diocese in England, with a couple of cars at his disposal, yet his reply was, "But, my dear boy, I am so grateful to you. I find it so hard to occupy my time here." He added that he was anxious to demonstrate that bishops are not really overworked. There are perhaps ways and ways of doing it. (What people mean when they talk about overworked bishops may be that the bishops are doing the wrong things, exhausting their time and energy in admin. at the cost of their pastoral and teaching office, trying to do everything with their own fingers. This

[7] Rather unlike another bishop of whom it is related that at lunchtime the butler came into the study announcing "Luncheon is served, my Lord" — and handed the visiting parson a plate of sandwiches.

attempt is likely to lead to a breakdown. But should a father-in-God be a lord-high-everything?)

When I go into a village church today, especially at a harvest thanksgiving, I find myself back in the atmosphere of my boyhood. But one thing is missing — the smell of oil lamps, which had come to have religious associations. (There are other religious smells, which in churches of a different type are found to be evocative.) The Church and the land are ancient partners, and village religion, despite all the changes, has been continuous since the pre-Christian era. Plenty of paganism still survives. It is the religion of christianised natural piety. The church in our time was packed on Sundays. The ringers pealed out their rhythmic changes, the choir 'rendered' its regrettable anthems, the congregation joined 'heartily' in the singing and listened attentively to the Rector's sermons. Worship was still a community activity, and the church was, as it still is, 'our' church. Going to church was the right thing to do. (Undoubtedly there was some illegitimate pressure, exercised through the tied cottage system; and the labourers were not communicants; that was something reserved for the quality. Yet even so, the proportion of communicants would be much higher than anything known today.) It was in some ways what it is often called, the golden age of the country parish. To all appearances here was a contented, sound, happy and Godfearing community. Beyond all doubt, there is something about the land which gives men depth and wisdom and stability and power to endure through the changes and chances of life. The countryman knows life at first hand, not at second remove like the urban masses, and he has a corresponding philosophy. But nobody with any inside knowledge will want to over-idealise village life. Pan has left a good many hoof-marks on it, and it can be divided and bedevilled by irrational feuds which seem to be ineradicable. Nor can anyone who grew up in the 'unspoilt', picturesque pre-war countryside, with its damp insanitary cottages and its toll of preventible yet permitted suffering, however nostalgic he may feel about it, really want to have it back as it was. Village life today is probably more healthy, spiritually as well as physically, than in its Victorian and Edwardian heyday; and, as many recent books have pointed out, commuters and immigrants have brought new life to it.

The moral scandal about the pre-war village was that those who produced the food were living themselves on the verge of starvation. Their diet was mainly potatoes, tea and cheap jam, and skim milk—which was thought to be rather luxurious. Again and again speakers recorded in *Akenfield*, and in similar books, recall, "We could never get enough to eat." The whole system was built on sweated labour. A boy's wage would be about fifteen shillings and a grown man perhaps earned a pound a week; and no one had heard of a forty-hour week or of overtime, though there would be some extras at harvest. And there was no other employment available. Many men joined the colours in peace and war as the one way open to getting sufficient food. The exodus from the country, however regrettable, was a real exodus from the house of bondage. Literally, the men worked themselves to death. What else could they do? For if they ceased working they lost their cottages, and there were no pensions, nothing but outdoor parish relief or the dreaded workhouse, in which old couples were inhumanly and wickedly separated. The golden age of British farming was an iron age for the labour force sustaining it.

What did the Church say or do about this? It did what it could. It helped the 'sick and poor' and tried to perform the bodily works of charity. But the poor to whom it was giving out doles, which might save a home from total disaster, were able-bodied men in full employment. This is scarified nowadays as paternalism. But what else could it do, in that situation? What else could the lady bountiful do? *Of course* ambulance work is not enough and not the full content of Christian charity. But should the Church leave the casualties to die because it is not able to stop a war? The Church was here confronted by social forces which no purely religious strategy could control. It needed forces, Christian in inspiration but secular and political in their working, to bring about any radical change. When the time came no body of men did more to bring the welfare state into existence than the clergy of the Church of England, under the leadership of William Temple.

The fact is, that not until quite recently has the Church had a social theology of its own. In the towns, at the industrial revolution, it accepted the *laissez-faire* philosophy and believed in the 'iron laws of economics' – fighting, as someone has nicely put it, to defend the historicity of Adam when it ought to have been fighting to defeat the economics of Adam Smith till F. D. Maurice talked about Christian socialism and protested that the whole competitive system was in contradiction to the laws of God. In the country, it accepted a near-feudalism as part of the divinely ordered scheme of things and did not ask the radical question at all. Most, if by no means all, of the country clergy were at that time dyed in the wool Tories and supporters of the land-owning interest. Again, what else could they be? They owed their existence to it; they depended on tithe, that is, on the price of corn, until Lloyd George's Tithe Commutation Act removed that irritant – to their financial loss. Joseph Arch, who attempted to organise agricultural workers, was spoken of as a kind of arch-fiend. He was 'out to make trouble' in the villages. Almost worse than that, he was a Methodist. (He had been an Anglican, but was driven out by revulsion at seeing how the Big House family was given precedence at the Communion rail.)

In that world, denominational differences were more social and political than religious. Church and Chapel were barely on speaking terms. If they met one another at all, which was improbable, Rector and Minister thought of one another not as fellow-workers in the vineyard but as rivals and dangerous competitors. Their ministries were largely directed towards keeping their respective flocks from straying into the wrong fold. Now that so few of the sheep are in any fold we are, thank God, more humble and more co-operative. In the ecumenical atmosphere of today things are increasingly taken for granted — shared churches, pastoral collaboration, interdenominational fellowship — that would at that time have been quite inconceivable. My friend Sir John Muirhead recalls an incident which well illustrates the then prevailing attitude. He was staying with us in one of our rectories and helping my father to mow the grass in the kirkyard. A man in a dog-collar passed — the Baptist minister — and Muirhead asked my father whether he knew him. The reply, in a shocked voice, was '*Of course* not.' He was perhaps rather more far gone than some; but the remark was by no means untypical.

My father stayed all the rest of his life in the country, first in three successive Norfolk parishes — Long Stratton, Denver and Swanton Morley — and finally at Bratton Fleming on Exmoor, a 'fair ground' if ever there was one. You could see Bideford Bay from the front of the house and the Bristol Channel from the bedroom windows. (No doubt it has now gone the way of all rectories and for aught I know may be a home for unmarried mothers.) He was never given any recognition, not so much as an honorary canonry, and no mark of episcopal appreciation. All his benefices were college livings. He laboured unknown and unrewarded. Towards the end of his life he was afflicted by a feeling of not being 'worthy' of preferment and of having been a failure in his ministry. But, though it is not what he might himself have chosen, he was almost the model of a country priest. Wherever he went he restored the church (raising the money singlehanded by writing innumerable begging letters) and rebuilt the school (sometimes opposed by the villagers). He was a devoted and untiring pastor, teaching in the school every morning, visiting the homes day by day, gathering the village boys round him and taking them, while he was young, for immense bike-rides. And he was a wonderful preacher in an earlier fashion. He had an astonishing power of retelling the Bible stories and making them seem contemporary — even Korah, Dathan and Abiram! I can hear him still passionately declaiming *These sinners against their own souls*; even though it is difficult to imagine that it was among the more urgent temptations of his rustic hearers to seek the Aaronic priesthood. (It is only now that we have come to realise that 'what the Bible says' has not always, if ever, a *direct* and untranslated message to twentieth-century men and women.) He had his limitations, like all of us; but he was a holy and dedicated man. He never failed to say the daily offices in the church, however many degrees below, and he spent hours in his study in prayer. (Confessing his sins, we children used to say, although he had so few sins to confess.) He took the lead in all village activities and he was a real father to the community. In all the parishes he served he is still remembered with respect and affection. But he never doubted, nor did his parishioners, that he had a right, as the duly authorised parish priest, in virtue both of his Order and his benefice, to take the lead and to lay down the law. And again, that is now suspect as paternalism, and all the progressives and some of the younger clergy want to undermine that position. This is one of the points at which, in my belief, progressive programmes are in fact reactionary. Nothing will shake my conviction, confirmed by experience, that the strength, and the future, of the Church in England (whatever the case may be in other churches) is bound up with the position of the parish priest. I have more to say about this in a later section.

II

School and University

IF I AM asked why I am a Christian, and an Anglican, and a
parson, the short answer would be, I suppose, "Because my father
was." Religion was in the air we breathed at home and we took
it in naturally and unselfconsciously. I have had to encounter
many doubts and questionings and have moved pretty far from
Victorian orthodoxy. In later life my father deplored my
tendency towards theological liberalism, but I owe to him the
fundamental faith which has enabled me to find the way
through, and the elements of personal religion, without which
theology has no *data*. He prepared me himself for confirmation.
I was confirmed in Long Stratton church by my godfather,
a College friend of his, Bishop Wallis, of Wellington, New
Zealand, and as I grew older he gave me some of the tools for
fashioning an intelligent belief. He was no doubt instinctively
conservative and to the end of his days never moved from the
position he held as a younger man. But at Cambridge he had
sat at the feet of Westcott. He was aware of, and bravely
adjusted himself to, the new, critical attitude to the Bible, and
he made no attempt to keep me in ignorance of it. He told me,
gently and half-apologetically, what was then commonly
described as the 'result' of Old Testament criticism. When the
same critical methods were applied to the Gospels, he branded
it as 'disloyal'. His main concern there was 'how to answer the
critics'. But *Lux Mundi* was published the year before I was
born; and though it was still regarded as dangerous he accepted,

however reluctantly, and taught me what Gore had written in
his famous chapter about the limitations of our Lord's knowledge. But neither he nor any of that generation really grasped
its radical implications. (It is far from certain that Gore did
himself.) They all held and handed on to us a basically docetic
Christology. It would have been thought blasphemous to suggest that the Lord's mind was historically conditioned, that he
asked questions to get information, that he thought and taught
as a man of his own time, or that he was, in any real way, a
man. (We were taught that he was not a man but Man — a
hangover from Greek metaphysics which seems to us now to be
almost devoid of meaning.) They did not believe in a real
Incarnation. The Christ in whom we grew up to believe was a
theological lay-figure. That is why a book like Glover's *The
Jesus of History*, old-fashioned though it now seems in retrospect,
came to us with such a shock of liberation — the Archbishop of
Canterbury wrote a preface to it! The recovery of a truly
human Jesus was no doubt one of the most important gains in
Christian thought in the last thousand years. The pendulum is
now swinging too far the other way.

All this, however, was still in the future. I was now moving
into adolescence and in 1903 I went to Bradfield, having won a
valuable foundation scholarship which, at that time, covered
most of the school fees. The headmaster was the redoubtable
H. B. Gray, who for reasons unknown was called Bart, and is
still remembered by that name in the legend. He was already
almost a legend. A short man with napoleonic compensations,
he was to Bradfield what Thring had been to Uppingham. With
creative vision and tempestuous energy, not unmixed with
personal ambition, he turned a small local choir school, started
by Stevens as rector of the parish, into a justly famous public
school. In it he was absolute dictator. It revolved round his
personality as its centre, and this was both its strength and
weakness. When I went he was still in his prime, though, partly
perhaps through a streak of megalomania, he was undermining

his nervous stability. At the end of my time he was beginning to fail and was on the verge of a mental breakdown. Even the boys were aware that something was going wrong. When he had to retire, shortly after, he left a terrible job to his successor, Harold Costley White, later Headmaster of Westminster, whom I came to know well when we lived in Little Cloister. My last sight of Gray struck me as tragi-comic. It was at my father's induction to Bratton Fleming. He was by then Vicar of Lynton, and after the service he was sitting patiently by the roadside waiting for the country bus that was to take him home – the conquering hero in a plebeian oxcart, not in the quadriga of Caesar at a triumph!

I had great respect and affection for Bart. (From force of theological habit I find myself always typing the word as Barth!) He took trouble with me and showed me much kindness, both as a boy and after I left school. At his best he was an inspiring teacher, who quickened our minds and enlarged our horizons. He admitted us, now and again, into his home. But he was very much The Headmaster, of a now bygone Victorian type, almost, indeed, The Doctor of *Tom Brown*. There was none of that easy personal relationship which has now so happily been built up by a later generation of schoolmasters. *Hoc volo, sic jubeo: stet pro ratione voluntas.* It went ill with anyone who disputed that.

The humanising and maternal element was supplied by an almost equally legendary and very noble lady, Ma Bullen, matron since nearly prehistorical times. By the time I arrived she had half-retired to Bridge House, which was a kind of nursery for new boys. She mothered generations of Bradfield boys, physicking them when they were sick, comforting them when they were unhappy, scolding them when they were ill-behaved. Of vast bulk, she had a terrific presence and was an untold influence for good. On Old Boy occasions she held court, and there are plenty of greyhaired men today who still rise up and call her blessed. She was the archetypal 'mother in Israel'. On her own territory she was invincible. Once she knew what she wanted, or what she thought was right, even Bart had to bow to her command.

When I was recently asked by a housemaster what the school was like in my time, I was tempted to fall back on Gibbon's phrase, the triumph of barbarism and religion. Barbarism partly in the physical sense — there was still a good deal of bullying and cruelty, and a new boy's lot was not a happy one. Barbarism also in the mental sense. Scholastic standards must have been fairly low, for I reached the lower sixth in my second year, and the whole ethos of the place was philistine. That was probably true of all public schools then. It was the heyday of muscular Christianity — compulsory games, which were good for 'character-building', and an anti-intellectual cult of athletics. We were never allowed a minute to ourselves.

The big idea was to keep the boys so occupied and leave them so tired that they would not get into trouble. Anyone suspected of any artistic interests could be written off as cissy or effeminate. Bart did what he could to counteract that. He encouraged all manner of 'societies', for music, for 'natural history', for Shakespeare, and, above all, he created the Greek Play. But even he could not overcome the *Zeitgeist*.

And religion. Bradfield was and is a church school. There were two compulsory services every day and full-dress Mattins and Evensong on Sundays, as well as the optional rite called 'early service'. This was simply part of the order of things and no one dreamt of its ever being otherwise. There was plenty of religion, all right. But if I ask, What kind of religion?, I should have to say that it was, in effect, the sacralising of public school ethics. Apart from Francis Paget, Bishop of Oxford, when he came to take the school confirmation, and he rather spoilt it by being so melancholy, preachers hardly ever preached the Gospel to us. They exhorted us to "take God onto the football field" or they gave us healthy advice about Christian manliness. (The sermons of the ordained staff were pitiful.) Bart's pulpit rhetoric set the spine tingling. But his sermons too often were sepulchral warnings against the Works of Darkness, 'secret

Vice', and awakened in us such fear and guilt as made adolescent masturbation a far more intractable problem than it need have been.

Certainly we learnt the book of the words in Divinity lessons, generally well taught, and I should not now wish to play down the value of sheer religious instruction. But how far was it Christian education? All schools are faced with that question now, in more acute form than Bradfield was then. Gray could still take churchgoing homes for granted. But the ultimate Christian questions never arose. We were not encouraged to ask ultimate questions. Indeed, we were very strongly discouraged from entertaining dangerous thoughts of any kind. We belonged to the professional class and the sober religion of the Church of England and were being educated to stay there; which, so far as it went, was perfectly true. The school was not maintained to produce rebels.

Bradfield gave us basic 'Christian knowledge', and something more than that. But I think, in retrospect, that perhaps its best and most permanent religious gift was not technically religious at all, but was due to unconscious influence emanating from the beauty of the surrounding Berkshire countryside. "Dull would he be of soul who could pass by" and remain entirely unaffected by it. Somehow it entered our spiritual bloodstream. ("Beauty born of murmuring sound/shall pass into her face".) It would have been hard to grow up in those surroundings without being permeated with "a sense of something far more deeply interfused" – the bluebell woods in May can be a theophany. It gave me a heightened sensitivity to and reverence towards natural beauty, and that is surely a gateway to faith and worship.

When I go back to Bradfield now, as I am most kindly invited to do, to my great enjoyment, almost every year, to preach in the chapel and talk to the sixth form, I realise how much kinder and happier and more civilised a place it is; and how much more religiously mature, even though it contains many more avowed agnostics. The questions the boys ask me are questions that I might just have been beginning to ask during my third or fourth year at Oxford. But, then, they are now encouraged to think for themselves. I am flattered by having been made the eponymous hero of the Barry Society, which exists for the purpose of theological discussion.

It is fashionable to condemn the public schools for having produced a class-conscious caste with narrow outlook and unoriginal minds. But with all their limitations and deficiencies the public schools of those days did produce an exceedingly fine type of 'prefect', who manned the Indian and colonial services, officered the armed forces, and provided the executive leadership in the professions and in public life. An imperial power *needs* a governing class, as is now being discovered in the USA. Without them, the world would have been the poorer. Times change, and new ideals are now dominant. But in practice today a comprehensive school may be more class-conscious than the public schools are.

Among my contemporaries at Bradfield with some of whom I kept touch in adult life (not many survived to keep in touch with) was the great Air Marshal Guy Garrod – plainly a great man even as a schoolboy. Several years junior to me there was a quiet little boy with blue eyes who became Air Marshal Sir Roderic Hill, and a close friend and parishioner in Westminster. His wife Helen is still a valued friend of ours. There were, too, the three brothers Hamilton, so closely knit a corporation that they always said 'we' rather than 'I', yet so different in themselves. They were Crewe, for long years a vicar in Hertfordshire and for some few months a colleague of mine in Egypt; (Sir) George Rostrevor, poet and civil servant; and Eric, who died as Dean of Windsor. There was also the famous Ronald Wingate, though I lost touch with him after he left Oxford, Admiral Lord Fraser of the North Cape; and, just to diversify the picture, Colin Edison, prominent in Christian Science.

In due course I began to grow up and became a prefect and got my first lessons in responsibility. I acted in the Greek play, the *Antigone*, playing Teiresias to Garrod's Creon – Teiresias, the ancient prophet, prophetic perhaps of the shape of things to come! My mind was beginning to develop, and though I never was a 'pure scholar' – 'scholarship', as I found out later, may be a substitute for thinking – I became pretty deeply imbued in the Classics. The 'grand old fortifying curriculum' was in some ways, no doubt, rather narrow. We remained completely illiterate in the sciences and totally ignorant of general history. Nor had we any knowledge of current affairs. But in my case it was narrower than it need have been. It was not the demand for university places, as it would be now, but parental poverty that forced premature specialisation on me. Bradfield offered me things that I did not accept. I could have had some knowledge of French and German; I could have known something about modern history; I might have browsed far more widely in the library. But I simply could not afford these luxuries. I knew that if I did not get a scholarship I should not be able to go to a university or hope to enter professional life at all. We had to earn our higher education! So all the possible trimmings had to be sacrificed. But my classical education admitted me to the world of *litterae humaniores*, with all its mental and spiritual treasures, and laid the foundation for all my future thinking. I can never be grateful enough for it. And here I record my special gratitude to two of my teachers in the sixth form. It was C. A. Vince, a distinguished classical scholar, who first taught me to love Greek as literature, not merely as schoolroom material for the doleful exercises of grammarians. "The object of all this," he would say, "is to help you to put your feet on the fender and read Homer because you enjoy reading him." My other debt is to Lester Irvine, who first taught me to love and to memorise English poetry. No man could give one a better gift than that.

In the winter of 1907 I won an open scholarship at Oriel. At the end of the summer term, when I left school, my father took me for a month to Mürren, where he had been given the English chaplaincy. (The cost, I believe, was borne by a fairy godmother.) This was my first sight of the blessed Jungfrau, and indeed the first time that I had crossed the Channel — an exciting and unforgettable experience. I went up as a scholar to Oriel in Michaelmas term, 1908.

2 ORIEL

So began my sixty years of membership in Oriel, the beloved alma mater. When Gray asked me what college I wanted to put down as my first preference in the scholarship examination, this was my choice. I knew nothing at all about it and had no considered reasons for choosing it. I must have been guided by some homing instinct. The moment I saw it I fell in love with it, and it was a great day in my life when it elected me. I am fortunate indeed to have been at Oxford in those golden years before the war, in which 'to be young was very heaven'. Nobody who is there today can begin to imagine that charmed atmosphere, before Oxford developed a guilt complex and, instead of pursuing its own excellence while broadening its social base, tried to turn itself into something else. Oriel was at that time a very small college (I think there were only ninety undergraduates) so that everybody knew everybody and everyone had to make his contribution. I was admitted into a brilliant year, nearly all of whom were to perish in Kitchener's army. Among the very few still surviving are my lifelong friend (Sir) John Spencer Muirhead, afterwards eminent at the Scottish bar and in civic and university life in Scotland, John Sargent who served with distinction in the educational service in India, and Brigadier Stephen Longrigg of Iraq fame. Just senior to us but up at the same time, were Weston Stewart, already a B.A., subsequently Bishop in Jerusalem and Eric Graham, afterwards Bishop of Brechin.

One of my contemporaries at another college (Brasenose) was the author and critic, John Middleton Murry, then an agnostic if not an avowed atheist. I met him quite often and kept in touch with him afterwards. Twenty-five years later when I was a Canon of Westminster he came to see me, now become a Christian, to announce that he wished to be ordained and to ask me to arrange a smooth passage for him. (That would have been a sensational event in the literary circles in which he moved and George Bell was greatly excited when I told him.) I secured for him an entry to Westcott House, but for whatever reason — I never knew — he withdrew at the last minute and nothing came of it. But it was rather a thrilling conversation.

The Provost then was the formidable Shadwell, a Dante scholar and a real old-fashioned Head of a House. Undergraduates had very little contact with him except when we were commanded to his dinner parties which were extremely alarming experiences. (The butler would come to one's room in the morning and say, "You will be dining with us tonight.") The Dean was F. H. Hall, a 'permanent deacon' —he had, I suppose, taken Holy Orders long before as the condition of his fellowship — who was something of a legend in college and an ailing man, but masterly at his job and always ready to help whenever he could. He showed me much kindness as my 'moral tutor'. The most colourful figure in the Senior Common Room was L. R. Phelps, subsequently Provost, already the hero of a Phelps saga, and perhaps the last of the Oxford 'characters', who, beneath his elaborately staged idiosyncrasies and eccentricities, was a deeply if rather shyly religious man, about as unclerical as a cleric could be. He had a pervading influence in the college, and with him I was later to be on intimate terms. (Many years later it fell to me to write his obituary in the *Oriel Record*.)

Ours was an almost exclusively male society. Women were not yet admitted to degrees, and their colleges had not been desegregated. Indeed, the girls lived almost in purdah. They were not allowed in a man's room in college, unless they were his sisters or cousins (some men acquired a remarkable number of cousins) and when they came to lectures they were chaperoned by matronly ladies from North Oxford, who sat and knitted and then marched them back again. And though, after school, we felt as free as the air, we were under a mild social and moral discipline such as students today would not tolerate. The colleges had not abjured responsibility for being *in loco parentis* to their young men.

In the smaller colleges of that period the tutorial system was an effective reality. The dons were interested in their pupils, they did not regard us as unwelcome interruptions to their own research. We were in constant touch with our tutors, and we got a full hour with them every week. I cannot adequately record my debt to the two men (both, happily, still living) who tutored me for Greats — to Marcus Tod, the eminent Greek epigraphist, and (Sir) David Ross, editor of Aristotle, who initiated us into philosophy. (They were always known as the Right and the Good, but with some uncertainty which was which.) Outside the walls of the college there were lectures by men of such quality as Gilbert Murray (then at his prime) on Greek tragedy and religion, Rashdall, Prichard, Joseph and Cook Wilson, to name but a few, on ethics and metaphysics, Zimmern and Haverfield and Ernest Barker on Greek and Roman history and politics, and Percy Gardner (known in another role as a leading 'modern churchman') on Greek archaeology. Under such stimulus and in such a climate my mind began to expand in all directions. But the most important educational instrument in a college is probably the Junior Common Room — undergraduates educate one another. The innumerable college societies to which we belonged gave me widening interests in the arts, in literature and in drama; and, incidentally, in preparing papers for them, I discovered that I could, more or less, write English.

Oxford was, no doubt, rather a walled-in garden, sheltered from the rude winds beyond itself. Nearly all of us came from professional homes — in my college at least there were very few exceptions — and, although the scholars at any rate had earned them, we took our privileges too much for granted. We had no very developed social awareness — that was to come in with the post-war generations. We had little knowledge or imagination of the hells beneath the surface of the establishment. But we were not without some social conscience within the limitations of our own time. We were beginning to feel some slight uneasiness. There was a solemn debate, at which visitors from the Working Men's College were speakers, on the motion that the working classes ought to be admitted to Oxford. (It was carried I think by a small majority.) But we were not ashamed of being middle class. We knew nothing of that inverted snobbery which seems to afflict so many undergraduates and junior staff in the present-day universities. Oxford tried to discharge its social obligations by running clubs and settlements in the East End; the most important of these were Toynbee Hall, Dr. Stansfield's Oxford and Bermondsey Mission, and the Oxford House in Bethnal Green, to which was due my first meeting with Dick Sheppard.[1] Quite a large number of undergraduates would stay in these and give help during vacations. Within the conditions of that time the Settlements certainly did a power of good.

On Whit-Mondays the clientele of the Settlements were invited up to Oxford in force. We showed them round, took them on the river and gave them tea in our rooms — and felt a glow at having discharged our social duty. Perhaps there was not much more then that we *could* do. Some of us belonged to the Christian Social Union, one of the children of Maurice's Christian socialism, which was presided over by Scott Holland, then a canon-professor at Christ Church. This tried to do something about conditions of labour, and provided us with lists of approved tradesmen guaranteed not to be paying sweated wages, particularly in the tailoring trades. But it could not or did not attempt very much more than that. Christian action had not then been heard of. Radical change was not yet on the map. (All the same, the great Liberal pre-war Government, perhaps the best Government in our history, was already passing social legislation which prepared the way for social democracy.) Of course, it was an élite society — I find it hard to

[1] When Dick was Head of Oxford House his father, Canon Edgar Sheppard, who was sub-Dean of the Chapels Royal, went to visit his son in the East End. By way of protecting himself against such perils, he arrived in a carriage guarded by outriders.

attach any meaning to non-selective higher education. Let it not be forgotten, however, that when the war came, that generation almost to a man flocked in its thousands to the recruiting offices, not grudgingly or of necessity, and supplied the leadership of the new armies. (The expectation of life for a second lieutenant once he reached the front was ten days.) They were conscious of a *debt* and, God knows, they paid it.

My religious life in these years was moving quietly in green pastures and beside still waters. I was not yet certain about ordination; but, apart from some thoroughly healthy doubts as the mental excitements of philosophy invaded my rather conventional theology, I felt quite secure in Christian fundamentals. I did not experience any dramatic crisis. Like many adolescents, I passed through a silly phase of ecclesiastical spikery, attending the more extreme Oxford churches and morbidly interested in ceremonial. It was something that had to be worked out of the system, and I very quickly got over it. Some men, unhappily, never do get over it, and go through life as religious adolescents. In the cradle of the tractarian movement a great many influences were in our favour. The regular services in the college chapel unconsciously steadied and sustained me. I enjoyed the friendship of many committed Christians. (I imagine that almost every man would have then described himself as a Christian and have been surprised if anyone asked the question.) Some of us went with reasonable frequency to the Sunday evening sermons in St. Mary's (for which I was later to become responsible) and listened, often thrilled, to the famous preachers. There was Queen Victoria's favourite cleric, Boyd Carpenter, Bishop of Ripon, with a fine style of oratorical piety such as we could not now endure, though I thought it wonderful at the time. There was Cosmo Lang, Archbishop of York, with his lovely voice and magnificent presence. And there was, of course, Winnington Ingram of London, the one man who packed St. Mary's to overflowing, whom Randall Davidson, not much given to lyricism, described in his early days in Stepney as "the greatest religious force since Wesley". He would preach at Radley in the morning, walk out to Oxford in the afternoon, preach in Keble chapel before dinner and reappear in St. Mary's at 8.30. There were devotees who went the rounds with him! I remember sitting spellbound in the gallery. (But many years later, when I was in his diocese, Ingram was still Bishop of London, still playing tennis on his lawn at Fulham, still repeating the old familiar sermons. At the end of his time he was pitiful to listen to.) Some of us also took some part in the far too many religious organisations competing for subscriptions and membership, and all doing very much the same things. Like a good many other 'religious' activities these were, I should now judge, rather a waste of time.

The four years were gone before we could count them. We took our final schools in June 1912, and the College scored four firsts in Greats. As we took farewell of him David Ross remarked, "You will soon forget all you have learnt, but there is one thing that Greats will have done for you. You will always know when a man is talking nonsense." We have not lacked opportunities for testing that. I reminded him of it a few years ago. He replied that he found it hard to believe that he had ever said anything so sensible.

But did we forget? Mere factual information tends, no doubt, to fade as the years pass; but that can always be checked from books when needed. What was remembered was something far more valuable. Our teachers had taught us how to think, and given us the desire to go on thinking. Through all my long theological odyssey it has been a quite inestimable advantage to have been initiated in student days into moral philosophy and metaphysics. The system of thought to which we were introduced is now, at least temporarily, out of fashion, and a bleaker philosophy is asking whether there is such a thing as metaphysics. (It has not yet asked why it asks that question; and when it does, its closed world may be opened again.) At our age, of course, we knew the answers better than we understood the questions – that can only come with experience of life. I knew what Kant said, and the right things to say about him,

45

but had not then grasped the implications of the Kantian revolution for Christian thought. But what remained, to be developed later, was at least a dawning appreciation of the moral argument for Theism. And in mature life I have never doubted that belief, unsupported by natural theology, is in a barely defensible position, or that any viable theology must be a philosophical theology. The study of ancient history and philosophy gave me some informed appreciation of the world in which Christian thought was moulded, and the key to the understanding of Nicaea and Augustine, to say nothing of St. Thomas, and of the growth of western Christian civilisation. I still believe that Oxford classical humanism is a quite first-class mental training for even an amateur theologian.

Since I now felt clearer about ordination, I applied for an extension of my scholarship and stayed up for a fifth year to read Theology. My supervisor was Richard Brook of Merton, afterwards Mervyn Haigh's archdeacon at Rugby, then Bishop of St. Edmundsbury and Ipswich. Thus began a friendship which lasted all through life till his recent death at the age of eighty-eight. I was nominated to one of the Liddon studentships, administered by Walter Lock, Warden of Keble, where he was known as 'The Crab'. That kind, learned and very cautious scholar had a secret rather like that of Samson's hair. So long as he could stand on the hearthrug with his back to the fire, he controlled the interview and was perfectly in charge of the situation. Undergraduates learnt that if they could upstage him and stand there first, he would be like clay in their hands.

In the course of this fifth year I was picking up a few minor University prizes. I was therefore able now, to my great relief, to finance myself out of my academic earnings without coming down on my father any longer.

The honour school of Theology at Oxford was almost entirely critical and historical. The idea was that if it remained objective, without involving questions of belief, that made it academically respectable. It stood alone, isolated from other disciplines. Alan Richardson has remarked somewhere that putting Theology under the Arts Faculty in the new universities has been a victory over both rationalism and ecclesiasticism. In my time it was largely preoccupied with the search for Jesus behind the Gospels and dominated by the synoptic problem. Sir John Hawkins' *Horae synopticae* is one of the monuments of that period, and Streeter's great book on the Gospels was in the making.

I learnt much from B. H. Streeter ('Struggins') who was afterwards to achieve so wide an influence through the books in which he attempted to bridge the gulf between Theology and the natural sciences. The Old Testament professor was Driver, and my future father-in-law, Buchanan Gray, though I did not know him at the time, was at work on his books, which are still in use, at Mansfield. William Sanday was Margaret Professor — a reverent scholar, much trusted by Anglicans, so determined to be open minded and not to get stuck in positions already won, that he would change his opinions, and say so, while his books were in process of being printed.[2] Scott Holland, that eager and fiery spirit, was giving lectures on the fourth Gospel, some passages of which I can still remember.

But those years just before the skies fell in were a time of great theological excitement. Textual criticism of the Gospels was making inroads on traditional formulas and inevitably seeming to undermine long established interpretations of the Person of Christ and the meaning of his 'divinity'. The trend was towards an English version of Modernism. And the bishops became extremely nervous about it. In 1911 J. M. Thompson published his then very radical book on Miracles. *Foundations* followed in 1912. These two books seem rather old-fashioned now, for theology is and must be always moving. But at the time

[2] Bishop Wand recalls how William Sanday once referred in a lecture to prayer. "Only one familiar with the period will understand how startling was a word of such personal religious faith on the lips of a theological lecturer." *Changeful Page* (Hodder and Stoughton 1965), p. 36.

their impact was hardly less than that of *Honest to God* in these later years. There were the usual protests and a clamour for the suppression of dangerous opinions and the censure, if not the removal, of their authors. Bishop Talbot, as Visitor of Magdalen, had withdrawn J. M. Thompson's licence. A cry was raised for the inhibition of Streeter on the ground of his views on the Resurrection appearances. Pulpits resounded with denunciation. I well remember a sermon by my father on the text: "They have taken away my Lord out of the sepulchre." (What *would* they have said about Professor Lampe's famous broadcast on the empty tomb?) Bishops were shy about ordaining men who had been tutored by Streeter or Rashdall. London was rather suspicious of Mervyn Haigh; and, strange though it seems now in retrospect, Paget of Oxford refused to ordain Temple, on the ground of some admitted reservations about the Virgin birth (not a denial of it). Indeed, had it not been for Randall Davidson, William Temple might never have been ordained and Henson might never have become a bishop. An attempt was made to force through Convocation a resolution which would have had the effect of condemning all liberal opinion and discouraging free scholarly research — and that would have been the end of the Church of England and its unique place in the Christian world. Sanday and others, of course, reacted strongly, and finally the Archbishop himself, whose peculiar distinction it was to have saved a divided Church from disruption and preserved its characteristic comprehensiveness, drafted a far more liberal form of words (see Bell's *Life*, ch. XLI).

So I was to begin my study of theology in an atmosphere of alarums and excursions, amid cries of betrayal and Why don't they resign?, complaints that our leaders had sold the pass, appeals to rally round the old flag, and all the familiar noises of controversy. These have continued, in one form or another, all the way through my active ministry. Thus the explosion of radical theology which has reverberated through the sixties, however perplexing to men of my age and training, did not alarm or worry me in the least. I have been through this kind of thing too often before — and heard too many of the 'new' catch words.

In that year and the next I began to have contacts with some younger dons who later became prominent and whose friendship remained till the end; such as John Rawlinson, afterwards Bishop of Derby, and (Sir) Walter Moberly (now the sole survivor of the collaborators in *Foundations*) subsequently Vicechancellor of Manchester and chairman of the University Grants Committee. From time to time I met Oliver Quick of Corpus, who was for a short while chaplain at Lambeth and then after holding canonries (surely a record) at Carlisle, Durham and St. Paul's, ended up as Regius Professor at Oxford. His religion, drawn from deep wells, and his subtle intellect, revealed in a number of influential books, gave him a unique place as a theological teacher.

At the end of that academic year (June 1913), after certain approaches from another college, Oriel elected me to a fellowship, with a year of grace in which to prepare myself, to serve as chaplain and tutor in Theology. This was beyond anything I had hoped for, and I looked forward eagerly to the prospect of teaching and pastoral ministry in the college. As things turned out, it was never to happen that way. I applied for ordination to Bishop Gore, who asked me whether I had any doubts, definitely expecting the answer No. For, as I have already said, the episcopate was then extremely nervous. (If an ordinand had told me, as a bishop, that he was unvisited by any doubts, I should have told him to run away and look for some.) I then settled down to acquiring more knowledge. A good part of the following year was spent in Germany. I sat at Wilhelm Herrmann's feet at Marburg — did I possibly see, without knowing it, Barth and Bultmann? — and afterwards 'heard' Karl Budde at Freiburg in Breisgau, and did something, I cannot remember what, in Weimar.

As required by the bishop, I put in a term at the theological college at Wells, of which the principal was Godfrey Parsons, afterwards Bishop of Southwark and then of Hereford, and a senior colleague on the Bench. The vice-principal was R. H. Lightfoot ('the little man'), shy, humble, saintly and very shrewd, who could make quite devastating judgements. He developed into a top New Testament scholar, one of the first in England to explore the dangerous waters of form-criticism. In so short a time Wells could not teach me a great deal. But I learnt some elements of religious discipline — which was much the best thing it could do for me — and some rudimentary techniques. (But I absorbed unconsciously from my father more than any formal instruction could offer.) It was there, too, that I first knew John Halet, all through life a close friend and counsellor, whom forty years later I persuaded to come and work with me in Southwell diocese.

A few months later I was ordained deacon by Charles Gore[3] in Cuddesdon parish church. (Candidates left the church in frock coats and toppers.) It is one of the privileges of my life to have been ordained by Charles Gore and consecrated by William Temple. I cannot now think that Gore was always right, but there are few men for whom I have felt such reverence. He was my first real father-in-God. He was a patrician and every inch a bishop. Yet he rather hated being a bishop and when he resigned he went out with the air of a schoolboy starting the summer holidays. Stern as a prophet yet playful as a kitten, a free-thinker yet an authoritarian (and even, but for the grace of God, a persecutor), he was many-sided and infinitely complex; but what shone out most was his love for his young men. Fifty years later the Dean of Westminster did me the honour of inviting me to give the Gore memorial lecture, where I offered my small tribute to the memory of this great, beloved and enigmatic man, who never, perhaps,

[3] Perhaps one of Davidson's few mistakes was the pressure he brought on Gore to leave Birmingham, where he was a civic hero, with a statue erected to him while still in office, for feudal Oxfordshire where he was unhappy and, because of his social opinions, rather at loggerheads with the country gentlemen.

quite knew what he wanted and could never be happy till he got it.

But this was June 1914. Two months later the skies had fallen in. The lights were going out all over Europe and the world was never to be the same again. Nearly all that gifted generation had been slaughtered before a year was passed. The war memorials tell their own story. The bitter arrow spares not the noblest. A voluntary system seems to entail that the finest spirits are the first victims. (The second war demonstrated that conscription can be less disastrous in its social consequences, as well as morally far more justifiable.) From that holocaust of a whole generation, the potential leaders in Church and State, England has never yet recovered.

I felt it my duty at first to hold on and try to shepherd the remnant of the college in a stricken and depopulated Oxford, inhabited chiefly by the halt and the blind. There were still a few able-bodied men about waiting for their commissions to come through or till they were old enough to apply for them. One of them is now the Right Reverend Lord MacLeod. But as the numbers sank lower and lower, and the casualty lists began to come in, I became impatient to be 'over there'. I did a short spell with the YMCA at a base in the Easter vacation of 1915, and after my ordination as priest, the college having granted me leave of absence, I was commissioned as an army chaplain. In the course of the Michaelmas term I left Oriel, hoping soon to come back in peace to a 'normal' life, but, in the event, never to return to it. No man who was involved in that experience came out the same man that he went into it. And it was, as, I think, happened to many others, in war service that I was to find myself.

III

The First World War

MY FIRST OVERSEAS posting was to Egypt. I was sent with a
unit of Territorials who had volunteered for foreign service but
with no idea where they were going. We were somehow packed
into one ship at Plymouth, and despite the discomforts and
hazards (we were chased into Valetta by a submarine) I found
the voyage immensely exciting. It gave me my first sight of the
Mediterranean, and the sense of travelling to some strange new
world. I had very little idea what to do; no one had given me
any kind of briefing. But I managed to take a few services on
board and to get around among officers and men. By the time
we put in at Alexandria I had established some kind of position
and was more or less accepted as part of the unit. We were then
sent off to Ismailia, headquarters of the Suez Defence Force
and were told that we were defending the Canal (absurdly
enough, at that time, from the western bank) against a hypo-
thetical Turkish attack.

Here we were on biblical territory and the clue for sermons at
church parades, which I found so baffling, seemed to be to
exploit that. Aided by Driver's commentary on Exodus in the
Cambridge Bible for Schools and Colleges — an improbable
source for church parade sermons — I was able to point to some
of the biblical sites ('this happened just over there') and to
indicate Sinai, visible over the water. To all this they listened
with interest and attention. It did not teach them much about
Christianity, but it may have helped them to think that the
Bible might have something to do with 'real life'. But they
needed more than knowing the route of the Exodus. What they
needed was somewhere to go. There was very little indeed for

the troops to do and hardly any amenities were provided for them. They were fed-up and they were too little occupied — and Egypt is no place for men in that state. What could a young untaught chaplain do about it? I was all by myself, there were no other padres; but I was coached and encouraged by my chief, the Principal Chaplain in the Middle East — who was Jarvis, subsequently Chaplain General — and began to make little ventures on my own account.

I managed to get some money from Headquarters and found an Egyptian in Ismailia who put up for me a large Arab-style tent, shaded under some palm trees nearby. Elementary furniture was acquired from somewhere and volunteers from the troops ran a canteen for us. I spent all the evenings there with the men and was thus brought into much closer contact. This little effort changed the whole tone of the camp. And it gave me a much needed confidence. I had lived hitherto a very sheltered existence and had hardly encountered human life in the raw, and I had been scared stiff at the prospect of living with 'brutal and licentious soldiery'. But I had now been taken into their hearts. Companies would wave to me as they passed. Lorry drivers would stop and give me a lift. Everyone I met smiled and seemed pleased to see me. I discovered that there was dormant in me something of what it takes to be any kind of leader. Indeed, I was in the dangerous situation of finding myself a 'popular padre' — which is mortally perilous to a young man's soul. The apprenticeship had not been a complete disaster.

This episode, however, did not last long. Jarvis asked me if I would go to France and transferred me to the eleventh division, which was resting and reforming in the desert, after evacuation from Gallipoli, where they had suffered appalling casualties. On reporting, I was greeted by a staff officer, who said, "You were at Shrewsbury House." This was the Brigade major, Gordon Elton, a superb soldier and a superb Christian, to whom it became my privilege to administer the Holy Communion every Sunday morning; for he rarely missed, whatever the conditions. (He was killed in the later stages of the war.) I was assigned to live with the 5th Dorsets, with whose adjutant I formed a close and still continuing friendship. He was a head-master, and in France we sustained our morale by quotations from Homer which applied to catastrophic situations. I was with this division for some weeks or months. I would sometimes go for long rides in the desert, and felt that haunting sense of a Presence, which gave me new insight into the Old Testament. And, having secured a few days' leave to Cairo, I got my first sight of the Pyramids and the Sphinx (then an event, now a package-holiday).

But it was not long before the division embarked. Having landed in France, we were sent straight up to the front and almost immediately to the Somme. I was with them in some terrible engagements, notably in the assault on Mouquet farm, in which about half my brigade was annihilated. I had never seen a dead man before, much less bloody bits and pieces of men, and as near as nothing I turned and ran. They thought I was brave, but in fact I was too innocent fully to appreciate the dangers! The real test of courage comes later, when a man's nerves are beginning to wear down. What needs courage and resolution then is not walking about in no-man's-land but managing to hold on at all. Towards the end of the war I would sweat with fear even in comparatively safe places; but I don't think anybody was aware of it.

I was not allowed to be with them very long, for I was trans-ferred to the 20th Division and made, to my astonishment, senior chaplain. So I had, still so young and immature, to try to master the first stumbling lessons in the handling and leadership of other clergy, all of whom knew a great deal more than I did. I became deeply attached to this Division, which had a magnifi-cent record behind it, and was with them in the massacre of Passchendaele.

I was also involved in the battle of Cambrai, when the tanks were used for the first time — after being exposed to enemy view for some weeks! — and thousands of horses were waiting behind

54

the line for the long-awaited breakthrough by the cavalry. For a mile or two the advance went like a field-day, but it then ground to a halt and the cavalry generals were once again disappointed. As I tried to get back to the shed which was called my billet, the general position was so ill-defined that I found myself on the German side of the line and walked down what I had thought to be a British road, followed, yard by yard, by a sniper, till I came to a (British) wire entanglement. It was raining, and I had picked up a German mackintosh and must have looked a very suspicious character; so there I was seized by some Indian cavalry and had much trouble in extricating myself. But at last I got home, exhausted but still alive. The German counter-attack was appallingly fierce. The original front line was overrun and the day was only saved by the Guards at Gouzeaucourt.

But nobody stayed long anywhere on the western front and in 1918 I was moved, much against my will, from the 20th Division and 'promoted' (though I thought it demotion, for I did not want an administrative post) to be DACG of the 13th Corps. There I managed to get (very slightly) wounded – an unusual feat at a corps headquarters – when a shell came through the window of my billet. (It was during the German assault on the 5th Army and the dreadful retreat, which has been so often described, before the counter-stroke and the final victory.) But having come alive through the perils of battle, I nearly succumbed, before the end of the war, to that virulent influenza epidemic which killed more people than all the fighting. My recollection is not very clear, but I dimly remember the MO coming into my billet and hauling me out of bed and plunging me into a tub of water. Under his care I recovered in due course and was sent down the line to a convalescent depot. Some twenty-five years later when I was a bishop, travelling north in a freezing wartime train, I recognised the man in the opposite corner as the doctor who had rescued me that night. We eyed one another in silence for some time, neither of us quite sure of our ground, till at length I said, "You and I have met before; last time, you saved my life; do you remember?"

"Yes," he said, "I recognise you now, but I am a strong Presbyterian, and if I had known what was going to become of you, I might not have done what I did."

I was still with the Corps when the Armistice was declared. Such, then, in briefest outline, was my war. No one is likely to want to know more than that about it, although in my own life it was a turning point.

Much has been written about the Western Front and its now scarcely imaginable horror. I make no attempt to tell the story again, though I often wish that the younger generation, who talk about 'their boring old wars', could realise what a ghastly price was paid, and paid twice over, by their predecessors, for the liberties which they take for granted and some few of them so irresponsibly abuse. What I want to emphasise here is something different. The social and religious revolution started on the Somme and in the Salient.

We young chaplains were 'thrown' into a ministry for which nothing in our experience had prepared us. I myself had only just been ordained priest, hopelessly ignorant and inexperienced, and should perhaps never have been allowed to go. But all of us, apart from a few regulars, came from academic or churchy circles, in which we had worked along traditional lines within an enclosed ecclesiastical world. Now we found ourselves called to serve a mass of men under intense moral and physical strain, to whom most of what we had been taught to preach seemed to be almost totally irrelevant. The war revealed to us for the first time and with a very heart-searching shock what we ought to have known long before – the results of the industrial revolution in the alienation of the workers, who were now the armies, from the life of the Church. (There was a solemn enquiry about this in a book called *The Army and Religion*, which supplied religious and sociological evidence which is still closely paralleled today in mass-observation reports like *Puzzled People*.)

At first we were worried about the superficial things like their bawdy language and their womanising. (What else did we *expect* was likely to happen when men, separated from their wives and in the highest condition of physical vigour, were subjected to intense sex-stimulation by constant exposure to violence and killing?) But we soon learnt that these *were* superficial. Our real problems were very much deeper than that. Religion apparently meant nothing to them. Was this something for which we should upbraid men who were enduring far more than we were? Or could there be something lacking in the religion? For we learnt in battle how splendid and how noble these apparently irreligious people were. How were these grand qualities related to the Gospel that we had been ordained to preach? We could not conclude, of course, that they did not need it: but what message had the Gospel for them and in what form ought it to be presented? And beyond all that, in so evil a situation, of which the devil seemed to be in control, how could we go on believing in God at all, as the Father of our Lord Jesus Christ? We had to face the ultimate challenge to faith, first for ourselves, then for the men to whom we had been sent to minister.

William Temple said shortly before his death that theology might have been claiming to know too much, and that we must learn to rebuild from the foundations. It is common form today, with the collapse of the metaphysical scaffolding of Theism, to say that we must start all over again. In our own small way we chaplains had to do that. We had to re-examine our fundamentals and to hammer out a working theology which could stand the test of battle-conditions and give men a faith that could overcome the world. Thus I received a baptism of fire. We may not have said anything very startling, and what we said might now seem old-fashioned. We may not have reached conclusions so radical as most theologians now take for granted. (After all it was fifty years ago and another world war has happened since then. But what made Clement Hoskyns think so radically?) But the chaplains were to have a decisive

influence on the thinking and practice of the post-war Church
— some were soon in high positions of leadership; and we did, I
think, introduce a ferment which has gone on working ever
since and is working still more disturbingly today.

Of course the chaplains were not alone in this. The clergy
working in the home parishes were faced with very much the
same strains through the challenge of suffering and evil, and, no
less than Karl Barth in Switzerland, had to question some of
their own axioms. I am saying only that the 'new theology' was
born in the fire and the earthquake of those years. It cannot be
accidental that both wars have been followed by theological
explosions and by a new concern to relate the Gospel to what
we now call 'secular' situations.

At the end of the war a group of padres compiled a book
called *The Church in the Furnace* — commonly known as 'The fat in
the fire'. No doubt it was half-baked and it may have been
arrogant. I had not set eyes on it for forty years. But someone
showed me a battered copy recently, and — though I have had
to go far since then, continually revising my theology, and am
still, I trust, able to learn new things — it surprised me to see
how much of what I should say now was already implicit, however crudely and impatiently expressed, in what I wrote then.
The next stage in its development was at Knutsford.

But many of us, I think, would have gone under or have
suffered shipwreck of their faith had it not been for the pastoral
care and guidance of the great and saintly Bishop Gwynne,
Father in God to a whole generation of young men. Whether
given directly by himself or made available for us indirectly
through B. K. Cunningham at the chaplains' school, it saved
many from mental or moral breakdown, and sustained us all in
our dangers and adversities. I have used the word 'saintly'
deliberately. For he made it easier to believe in God, which I
take to be of the essence of sanctity, and he exercised an out-
flowing love and goodness which drew out the best in anyone
who had contact with him. When he appointed me a senior
chaplain and I ran into my first batch of difficulties, I told him

that the job was beyond me and asked to go back to my brigade. He said: "I am behind you." And that was enough. Wherever he went he brought strength and courage.

Yet in all my life I have never encountered anybody less like a saint in painted windows. A burly man, and a Welsh footballer, he was every inch masculine, a man's man. Yet he was patient and gentle as a mother. In early life he had been an incumbent in Nottingham where his name was still magic fifty years later. Among his friends and parishioners at Emmanuel, which was then uptown rather than downtown, were J. D. and W. G. Player, and his work as a missionary in the Sudan was generously supported by Navy Cut tobacco. He went as a chaplain with Kitchener's Nile expedition and after the battle of Omdurman he stayed there, to develop his apostolic mission and become in the end bishop and uncrowned king. When our war broke out he served as a fourth-class chaplain — I suppose, with troops sent from the Middle East — till Kitchener made him Deputy Chaplain General (he was always known as 'the DCG') — which at once raised the status of the Department and got it properly recognised by the Top Brass. (He had known some of the Army commanders when they were subalterns serving in the Sudan.) He made himself felt all over the Western Front; what he did for his chaplains can never be told in words. With a childlike faith and simplicity in his heart, in practical affairs he was shrewd and tough and was not to be taken in by the plausible. And he had an endearing, sly sense of humour. One time when he came to take a service for me, I was trying to help him into his rochet and chimere. "You seem," he observed, "to be rather better at dressing bishops down than at dressing them up" — the point of that remark will appear shortly. He was a beloved father figure, surrounded by a growing saga about his foibles and idiosyncrasies. On the administrative side he was served by able and devoted ADCs, among whom was John Macmillan, a chaplain at Lambeth on loan, and afterwards Bishop of Guildford. The DCG lived in a villa at Paris Plage, within easy distance of GHQ. There he had to entertain many visitors; but he did not allow that to consume his energy. After dinner he would shamelessly fall asleep, and leave his staff to cope with the VIPs.

When the war ended he was a national figure, and could have had any preferment he liked in England; and had he accepted an English diocese he would have brought a tired and dispirited Church a galvanic and creative touch as leader of the demobilised armies. But he stopped his ears against all the charmers and went back at once to 'my flock' in the Sudan, where he remained for the next thirty years. (This was not by any means my last contact with him, as will appear in subsequent parts of the book.) To many, Gwynne is no more than a name now; and it is hardly possible to convey to any who did not know him personally the impression he made on those who had that privilege. He was a commanding figure in that period; and his place is on the roll of the Church's heroes.

When the padres first went out with the BEF, the army had little idea what to do with them. In battle, they were left behind at the base and were not allowed to go up to the fighting front. What on earth, it was asked, could they do up there? A colonel would say "No work for you today, padre," meaning by that, no corpses for burial. The chaplains' job was to take church parades, on such rare occasions as these were practicable, to run entertainments, to help in censoring letters, and in general to act as welfare officers, thereby helping to keep up morale. But was that what they had been ordained to do? Some of the younger clergy today seem to be asking that question in reverse. The parochial ministry of the Church, they say, offers them nothing worthwhile to do. Better to turn themselves into welfare workers on a purely secular, humanistic basis.

By the time we arrived all this was changed. The chaplains were allowed to move freely everywhere and when the units 'went up' we went with them. Several were awarded VCs, and a substantial number were killed in action. (I lost two at Gouzeaucourt.) We would give Holy Communion in the dugouts, minister to the wounded and dying, share, so far as we might, in what the troops endured. (But we did not share the worst thing of all that those kind and often sensitive men had to suffer: we did not have to kill other human beings.) We did what we could to serve them in Christ's name – and surely the distribution of cigarettes was a relevant form of the cup of cold water – and they understood that this was why we were doing it. They did not regard us as just welfare officers. In some dim way they discovered that they needed what the ministry of the Church sought to offer. (As a senior chaplain I got used to hearing, "Of course all padres are washouts, but we are very fortunate in ours, and I don't know how we could get on without him." When that had been said to one in every unit, one began to wonder just who were the washouts.) It may fairly, I think, be claimed that the Department did something to re-establish the clergy and – far more importantly – what they represented in the respect and affection of the workers. Even today the opinion polls grade the social value of the parson above that of anyone else in the community. He still has a wonderful chance – if he would believe it.[1] Might we or could we have done more afterwards to lead the men back into the Church? That is bound up with many other questions. (But why was it ever supposed that a horrible war, with its slow coarsening of the moral fibres, would lead to a major revival in religion? Was it not almost bound to do the opposite?) Was the Church the kind of Church that would attract them? And that was only one factor in the whole problem. The question about religion after the war was part of the very much bigger question about England itself after the war. And the armies were beginning to ask that question. It was one that the chaplains could not evade.

The war dragged on with its ever-mounting casualties and the strain was telling on everyone involved. The troops were

[1] David Martin remarks that the clergy persuade themselves that they are unpopular almost as easily as doctors persuade themselves that they are underpaid. *The Religious and the Secular* (Routledge and Kegan Paul, 1969), p. 121.

tired and increasingly browned off. To what purpose, they began to ask, is this waste? Why are we being sent out there to die – the forces by now were predominantly conscripts – for a lot of plutocrats sitting at home at ease? (The effect of the Russian revolution on army morale was alarming the authorities.) Total war, in the vile modern style, probably puts a heavier strain in fact on the civil population than on the fighting men. And the drawn-out years of anxiety and bereavement, the incessant labour, the hardships and restrictions, were leaving the people at home very tired – and this affected the Church like everything else. When we think about the aftermath of the wars we do not perhaps make enough allowance for the sheer fatigue that followed when they were over, and the urgent desire to relax any kind of effort. But the armies did not properly understand what the home population was going through. (I was shocked, when I went on leave, to discover how short of food and elementary comforts my parents were in their Norfolk rectory.) There developed a very dangerous form of 'We and They' – the soldiers and the civilians – and a deep distrust of 'the politicians'; and the chaplains were not immune from that. We too were getting tired and 'frustrated' and developed our own version of 'We and They' — the chaplains at the front and the home Church. We tended to blame everything on 'the system' and particularly on 'the bishops', always the whipping boys of dissatisfaction. (Hence the remark about 'dressing Bishops down'.) Harry Blackburne, afterwards Dean of Bristol, then ACG at Horne's headquarters, was grossly rude to Archbishop Davidson when he bravely came out to visit the armies. "The bishops are sitting like a lot of old hens on eggs which they do not know how to hatch." Randall could not make head or tail of it, though he did his best by conferences with chaplains and by sending out emissaries and literature, to reassure them about the situation. It cannot be said that the Church officially was presenting a very convincing image. Convocation's contribution to the war effort was to spend these years in prolonged debates about reservation and the use of vestments

('Getting ready for the men coming back'!), finally to announce
to a war-torn nation that henceforth the celebrant at the
Eucharist might lawfully be dressed in a white alb plain. There
was some excuse for our discontents. It is one of the character-
istics of the clergy, and indeed of the Church of England as a
whole, that when they are faced with fundamental questions
they run away into secondary issues, following the line of least
resistance, and take refuge in administrative programmes.
Change 'the system' and 'God' will look after himself! (It is
happening again at this very moment.) A number of chaplains
took a great oath, which they published in a manifesto, that
they would not go back to work in the parishes till certain conditions had been fulfilled. I cannot remember what the conditions were, but all of them, almost to a man, did go back. We
were young men and we may have been swollen-headed and we
probably said a great many foolish things. But in these con-
spiracies and discontents was the germ of the Life and Liberty
movement, which finally led to the Enabling Act.

But a very great deal more was at issue than retooling
ecclesiastical machinery. The question was: What is the
Gospel really *about*? Only an other-worldly salvation? The
troops were asking radical questions now about the social and
economic structure which they were supposed to be fighting
to preserve. Were they worth preserving? Ought they to be
preserved? (When they saw from papers like *The Tatler* the
goings-on of wartime 'society', the marvel is that they did not
become murderous.) Must the war go on to defend that kind of
country? Why should they be submitted to all this to perpetuate
a society of privilege and of far too glaring inequalities of
wealth, education and opportunity? This was where the social
revolution started. Nothing could ever be quite the same again.
And these were men who had guns and knew how to use them.
They were not merely an army debating club.

The chaplains did what they could to guide these questionings. Towards the end of the war we developed an extensive
educational programme — a sort of secular version of padres'

hours — on social and economic affairs with a candour and openness of speech such as no army had been allowed before.[2] Tom Pym, afterwards Head of Cambridge House, was the original sponsor of this effort, which was strongly encouraged by the DCG, and, rather to our surprise, by GHQ. (Perhaps it seemed to them quite a useful way of diverting the men from forming soviets — though in fact that is how we dubbed our own efforts.) It may not have come to very much. How could it? But at least it got a good deal of steam let off, and may perhaps have helped some men to ask themselves what some of their slogans and catchwords really meant. But it also helped them to see that the Church might be their ally and not their opponent in pursuing their demands for social justice.

But the social and the religious revolution were really two aspects of the same movement. For we chaplains were forced to ask ourselves what were the religious meanings of all this ferment. Had the Gospel itself nothing to say about it, about labour conditions, housing, education, about the enhancement of human rights and dignity? Was not Christianity something about human life as God wills it to be, and the Lordship of Christ, not in the Church only, but in the whole social and economic order? Could it be exhausted in churchy activities? Thus this war, like the second, was followed by a re-emphasis on the social Gospel, which contained the seed of 'secular' Christianity.[3]

Shortly after the Armistice was declared, I received instructions to leave 13th Corps and 'proceed' to report at the DCG's

[2] Where we got our facts, or the books, I cannot imagine. Perhaps from the army education officers — but would they have carried literature of that kind? We may have drawn on some Lambeth reports which had been commissioned by the Archbishop on the Church and social problems. (See Jasper's *George Bell*, p. 24.) I remember that George Bell had shown me some of these when I was blowing off to him (on leave) to prove how 'advanced' the thinking of the Church was!

[3] The connexion between the war and the revolution (which it took the second war to put into effect) has been well brought out by Mr. S. Mews in an unpublished thesis on the effect of the war on the clergy of the Church of England, which he has kindly allowed me to read.

house. During the war, as I have related elsewhere,[4] Toc H and the vision of P. B. Clayton had inspired an attempt to collect the names of men who hoped, if they survived, to offer themselves for ordination. The time had now come to trace them and follow them up. This, in conjunction with several other people, was to be my assignment at Paris Plage. It involved some weeks of hectic office work, searching through masses of files and correspondence and slips of paper torn out of notebooks, and studying the secret Orders of Battle to discover to what formation units belonged and how communication could be established with the men concerned, if they were still there. As part of the plans for demobilisation, the Army authorities had prepared a scheme for setting up a number of schools in all manner of trades and professions in which men could be re-trained for civilian life. The DCG had obtained a promise that men 'volunteering for the Church' — a wonderful phrase — should have a school of their own, which would be in charge of the Chaplains' Department, and a camp had been assigned for it at Le Touquet. The collection and sorting out of names was the preliminary to taking it over. Meanwhile, the Home Church, faced with this unknown intake, not only from France but from all the theatres, and from the Navy and Merchant Service as well, had decided, though the plans were still inchoate, to set up some kind of *ad hoc* school or testing-place for the new 'service candidates'. Whatever shape this might take eventually, the school in France could give some pre-training for it.

When the paperwork was nearly finished Gwynne called me into his room and told me that I was to take charge of Le Touquet. Nothing of the sort had crossed my mind. I went out in the morning and wandered about the sand dunes, praying, as seldom before or since, for support and guidance in a responsibility for which I felt so pitifully inadequate. But Gwynne's decision, little though he realised it, was to redirect the future course of my life and lead me along unexpected paths.

[4] *Mervyn Haigh*, pp. 67 and *passim*.

The bishop conjured a teaching staff into existence from chaplains who had been dons or schoolmasters, some of whom came on with me to Knutsford; men were hurriedly summoned to 'proceed' to Le Touquet; and we took the camp over. I was in command of that unit. But as chaplains are not executive officers my official title was Chief Instructor[5] and I was advised by a military adjutant — rather as rajahs, in colonial days, were 'advised' by a British Resident. In that camp there was no sergeant-major. This was a pre-pre-theological college, while still answerable to the army for good conduct and military discipline. This involved a rather delicate balance, and methods had to be worked out *ambulando*. We gave lectures on whatever we could remember of whatever any of us happened to know, all improvised and without any books. Of course it was hopelessly amateurish. All we could do and all we were trying to do was to help the men's minds to reawaken and to find healing and recuperation in an atmosphere of friendship and happiness, within a framework of regular worship. Little more could be done on that side of the Channel.

Now that the fighting was over, the authorities encouraged (or anyway permitted) a number of eminent ecclesiastics to come over and visit the troops. Some of them came to Le Touquet en route.

One of the first whom I had to entertain was a Canon Garbett of Portsea, half of whose curates must have been in uniform. This was the beginning of a valued friendship which lasted for forty years and more through all the stages of his career, till I said goodbye to him on his deathbed. He will come into my story again and again. But the great event, and one which was decisive for much that was to come in the Church of England, was the visit of Archbishop Davidson. The Archbishop gave an address to the school and a note written down at the time by one who was present recalls the impression that he made on them:

[5] Hence the title 'the Chief' at Knutsford, by which I am still known to many elderly clergymen.

Surely the Archbishop was the very embodiment of his own message. We knew, of course, without seeing him, that his responsibilities were great, but when we did see him we could almost *feel* the burden he was bearing. As he faced us to begin his address, pausing first for a few moments, one saw the great seriousness of his demeanour – his manly bearing and quiet self-possession – and to many of us came the thought, What tremendous responsibilities he has. In a moment he had confirmed that thought by his opening words: "You are sharers with me in the tremendous responsibilities of these days." That sentence contained the burden of his message to us. "Each of you have a tremendous responsibility upon him, not only because of the peculiar opportunities of the calling which you are preparing yourselves to follow, but because of the greatness of the times, because of the deep significance of the foundations, which must now be laid on the ruins of a broken civilisation."[6]

It was here that after the most searching questions, he signed and handed to me his famous 'pledge', that henceforth no man accepted for ordination by competent authority after due testing, should be debarred by lack of means from training. This was a momentous decision, which not only opened the gates for all these students – state grants, of course were not yet available – but was in the passage of time to change the whole shape of the Anglican Ministry.[7] CACTM grants started at Le Touquet.

This meant that the projected school could definitely be started in England; and here we had scores or hundreds of men waiting for it. Tubby Clayton went home with an urgent assignment to find some place, somehow, somewhere, in which such a school could possibly be housed and, as is now part of church history, acquired the empty prison at Knutsford – an improbable place, but it was that or nothing. It was now conveyed to me that the two Archbishops wished me to be Principal

[6] From the *Le Touquet Times*, which I owe to the Rev. E. R. Wildbore.
[7] I wrote something about this in *Mervyn Haigh*, pp. 55, 58.

of the new school. There seemed now to be very little point in keeping the men any longer on the French side, where at best they could be only marking time. So I demobilised the whole lot and marched them down for the last time to railhead. Then I was given my own discharge by Gwynne. Six weeks later I met them again at Knutsford. We moved out of the desolation of war to the miracle of an English spring and summer.

So here was a vast new responsibility; and I had not yet reached my thirtieth birthday.

IV

Knutsford and After

I THE ORDINATION TEST SCHOOL

SIX WEEKS WAS a very short time in which to cope with the preparations involved in creating a new institution *ex nihilo*. The filthy and half-derelict building had to be made at least possible to live in. Furniture and domestic equipment had to be amassed from wherever it might be got. (The beds did not arrive until the last moment and each man had to carry his own up from the goods yard. But they were accustomed to worse 'fatigues' than that.) And above all we had to assemble a teaching staff of a quality on which everything would depend. A nucleus had come with us from Le Touquet, the rest had to be sought out and recruited. In the end Fortune or Providence provided us with a brilliantly gifted Senior Common Room, whose teaching is still remembered with gratitude by many elderly clergymen fifty years later. With a wonderful eagerness and adaptability these men threw themselves into the venture of devising new techniques for an operation in which there were no precedents to guide us. They had to discover how to teach adults, of whom many had only primary school behind them, things which they themselves had learnt in the fifth form. For the Church had started, without being aware of it, a pioneer educational experiment. It had been envisaged as a 'test school', to separate the grain from the chaff on evidence of educability. In the event it became something more than that. It was the first College of Further Education. When later, at our request, it was inspected, the report sent in to the Board was enthusiastic; and

Whitehall may have learnt something from the Church. In the evolution of ordination training, its lineal descendant is Brasted, where — as I learnt to appreciate as a bishop — they know how to perform intellectual miracles.

The school could not have existed, or continued, but for the organisation behind it — as it were, the lines of communication staff — and in particular to two men whose names ought not to be forgotten. The first of these is Canon Frank Partridge, Secretary of the Central Board of Finance, a financial wizard with top-gear driving-power, who forced through against all doubts and difficulties the grandiose project of Church House in Dean's Yard, where the Partridge Memorial Hall commemorates him. (Whether this was a blessing or a curse is still perhaps a debatable question. For once it had a vast central building the Church embarked on a centralising policy.) He supported us enthusiastically, raising money with gigantic energy and always giving the school what it needed. Afterwards he became Bishop of Portsmouth.

The other was Canon F. C. N. Hicks ('Bumbo') who in earlier life had been a tutor at Keble, and commanded the Oxford OTC (he was a remarkable figure in the saddle!) and then Principal of Bishops' College, Cheshunt. He now took over the laborious job of administering ordination training and became the chief architect of CACTM. He supported and guided us through all our troubles, and the school had no more devoted friend. Bumbo was to end his days as Bishop, first of Gibraltar and then of Lincoln.

So we opened our doors and the first batch of men came in. Now that we had them, what were we to do with them? We might hope to learn methods as we went along, but we had to be pretty clear about our objectives; and if I did not lead nobody else would. A weight of responsibility lay on my shoulders. I had to deal with all sorts and conditions of men, from senior commanders to full privates, and could hope to manage the personal relationships. But I lacked much of the knowledge and experience which my responsibilities demanded, and inevitably I made mistakes, some of which come back to my mind and torment me still. In particular, I did not know enough — and perhaps not many clergy at that time did, however much older than me they were — about the unconscious workings of the psyche, to help the men properly on the hard journey, beset by so many and great dangers, from war neuroses to pastoral maturity. Foreseeably, there were some disasters — not many; if any were my fault may they be forgiven me.

But I was not alone. I had the support and advice of a staff who never kept anything back from me. In the early days I leant very heavily on the guidance of F. M. Sykes — 'Syko' in the army, 'Psycho' to us — who had been my wise counsellor at Le Touquet and had now agreed to come with me as vice-principal instead of going back to his parish. Florid and heavily built, a bluff Yorkshireman with a fund of north country stories, he was a devoted and experienced priest, whose influence permeated the whole campus. He delighted, as a committed anglo-catholic, to shock the ecclesiastically minded out of forms of piety less robust than his own. Till Lang called him away to St. John's, Middlesbrough, where he died during Temple's primacy, he was the shadow of a great rock. On the educational side I was much helped by R. H. Burne (later Archdeacon of Chester and historian of Chester cathedral) who, as senior tutor, organised the teaching. In the office work and administrative detail I was able to rely on the devoted and invaluable service of Aubrey Hooper, who later became headmaster of a prep. school and is now retired from a Dorsetshire incumbency. My debt to Mervyn Haigh is related elsewhere.

There were others, like Leonard Browne and G. L. Heawood, and ever so many more. It would be boring to give a list of names. But in fact we were all learning from one another, staff and students engaged in the same quest. For the salient fact about life in Knutsford prison is that it was a *koinonia* experience. With a tragedy shared in common behind them and a common hope and expectancy before them — the pattern of Cross and Resurrection — they could hardly avoid being welded into a close and exhilarating fellowship. It was almost the New Testament situation. No ground could possibly have been more favourable for building up a dynamic community.

I found it impossible to make the time to take part in any regular class-teaching, though I gave private coaching to some of the brighter boys, one of whom became Fr. Charles Preston of Cerne Abbas, and attempted to introduce them to Plato. But I kept the R.I. in my own hands, and this was my main impact on the school. In the first period every day of the week I lectured to the whole school assembled, and put into it all I had to give. Ostensibly it was biblical exposition, with the aim of making the Bible come alive for them. But in fact I was telling them everything I knew and everything I wanted them to believe about the real meaning of Christianity and its relevance to the contemporary world. Some, I am told, still remember those hours; but I think I learnt from them more than I taught others.

But as my hearers were a large section of the post-war generation of clergy, what I tried to say then reached, inevitably, into circles far beyond the Hall in the gaol. Some of those theological insights by which, as I have described elsewhere,[1] Mervyn Haigh and I were beginning to be visited, penetrated into the Church at large. It would be grotesque to suggest that two young men trying to find their theological bearings after a cataclysmic experience changed the theology of the Church of England. But I think it is true that there dates from that period a move towards a new theological realism — for whatever could survive in those years, it could not be a sentimental theology — and a wider vision of Christianity in its bearings on secular affairs; and some seeds of this may have been sown at Knutsford.

It seems to be easier to arm the clergy against the grosser assaults of the ghostly enemy than to cure them of their addiction to party labels. Are you a 'catholic' or an 'evangelical'? Do you belong to Us or to Them? This gave some difficulty when

_____
[1] *Mervyn Haigh*, pp. 67 and *passim*.

the school started. These were men of all shapes and colours of churchmanship, all of whom had been starved for years of worship, and at first they tended to want to hive off and indulge in esoteric rites of their own in accordance with their sectional allegiances, in private conventicles of their own devising. This threatened a seriously disruptive force. But we had to learn how to live and worship together in a richer and more inclusive community, in which our manifold differences of churchmanship were not just ironed out, but enriched and complemented in mutual trust and understanding. A large number of ordinands began to learn a new tolerance and comprehensiveness which was bequeathed to the next generation and became the possession of the whole Church, and may perhaps be claimed to have held within it some of the seeds of the ecumenical movement.

In the spring of 1969 it was half a century since Knutsford opened, and many who had begun their training there expressed a wish for a jubilee reunion. Leonard Wilson, Bishop of Birmingham — one of its products of whom we are most proud[2] — procured us the use of St. Peter's college, Saltley. There assembled there a body of grey-haired clergymen, all, in the nature of things, over seventy and most of them by this time retired — Old Boys who really were old boys, some of whom I had not seen for fifty years and found it extremely difficult to recognise. We must have looked like an exhibition of ecclesiastical antiquities. It was a joyous reunion of friends for all of us, and to me a deeply moving occasion. That brave experiment which the Church has made had sent out hundreds of clergy to staff the parishes[3] — and only that new intake of ordinands saved the parochial system from collapse — and into the wider Anglican Communion, for I had met Knutsford men all over the world. But I felt then that, in the providence of God, the

---

[2] There were at least three other bishops: Ambrose Reeves (Johannesburg) Harold Beardmore (St. Helena) and George Clarkson (Pontefract, afterwards, Dean of Guildford).

[3] There are about 450 priests in active work or recently retired who began their training at Knutsford.

school had been allowed to do something more than that — to send out some new spirit, some new vision, into the thought and life of the Church of England, both in its homeland and far beyond it.

The school lived in a glare of publicity and was headline news in the Church while it lasted. Scores of VIPs came to visit us, and I myself had to go all over the country giving talks about it and helping Partridge to raise the funds. This forced me into a premature prominence, and gave me access to exalted circles which would otherwise never have been open to me. Thereby it led me into a future ministry quite other than anything that I expected.

There were plenty of extra-mural activities. One of them, specially difficult and important, was to be asked to share with Bishop Mike Furse in a mission to Cambridge university. My addresses were to be given in Holy Trinity, of which Edward Woods was then vicar. I could only do this kind of thing in my own way, not to a pattern prescribed by anyone else. As I began to get into my stride the first evening, Edward came up into the pulpit and said, "This kind of thing will never do. You must tell them stories and speak in such a way as to be understandable by my cook." In the brief, tense dialogue that followed I tried to explain that on this occasion I was not addressing his admirable cook, but trying to reach out to the university. After that I went on again in my own way. I can only say that the undergraduates did listen, and seemed to listen rather intently. Among my hearers, though I was quite unaware of it, and at that time altogether unknown to me, was a girl from Girton — to whom this book is dedicated.

One other episode of that week remains with me. At that time at Knutsford I was doing a certain amount of cross-country running with the young men, and was asked to join in a run with a Cambridge side. I felt that this might not be wholly irrelevant to what I was trying to do at Holy Trinity. So I accepted, only to discover that this was a picked team in high training. But I could not draw back then, and had to go through with it. I did get home, in a state of exhaustion, and not too disgracefully low, either. Whether this did anything to foster the defence and confirmation of the Gospel, there was, of course no means of knowing. But I noticed that all the team were in church that evening.

At the end of the war I was still a fellow of Oriel, and with every intention of going back to my duties there. But when the Archbishops sent me to Knutsford I felt bound to stay with it and see it through, and one could not know how long that would be. The college gave me further leave of absence, but one could not keep them waiting indefinitely. So, though it was a painful step at the time, I felt it my duty to resign my fellowship, and the way back was now closed behind me. I stayed at Knutsford for nearly four years in all. But in due course the school began to run down, and when the numbers had dropped from three hundred or more to thirty or forty, I felt that perhaps the time had come to move on. But where would be the 'fresh woods and pastures new'?

At this point I was strongly pressed by Bishop Gwynne to go to him as archdeacon in Egypt and in charge of his cathedral in Cairo. Again, it was not in the least what I had expected, and never in my wildest dreams, or nightmares, had I imagined myself as an archdeacon. But as I was still an unmarried man, it seemed to me that a call overseas ought to be regarded as authoritative. And in any case, I was far too fond of him to refuse to do anything that he might ask. We had learnt to accept his wishes as imperatives. So I offered my resignation to the Council and took my leave of the Knutsford remnant.

2 EGYPTIAN INTERLUDE

When I told the Archbishop about Egypt he replied that I was to go and discuss it with him. I discovered then that His Grace was not amused. He said he regarded it as a great mistake; it was not the work that I ought to be doing at all. There were far bigger opportunities for me in England. But none, I ventured to say, had been suggested to me, and in any case I had given my promise to Gwynne, and it had in fact been already announced. Very well, then, I could go for the time being; but it must be on the clear understanding that it was to be only a temporary interlude and that I was to come back as soon as possible. This was rather damping to my young enthusiasm. The Archbishop then went to the telephone, and told me that there was an important teaching post now vacant at King's College, London, and instructed me to put in an application for it. If I were elected (and, in my own mind, nothing seemed less likely to happen) I was to return in time for Michaelmas term. The Bishop would shortly be coming home on leave and he would himself put everything right in that quarter.

Under these rather inauspicious omens I sailed again down the Mediterranean and came back, in an unexpected role, to Cairo. At Bishop's House, where I was to live, adjoining the old Anglican cathedral, I found already established two friends — my old schoolfellow Crewe Hamilton, a regular member of the cathedral staff, and John Halet, then a curate at Portsea, who was convalescing from an alarming illness. We three formed a very happy community, looked after by a French-speaking cook of indeterminate nationality and a perfectly trained Sudanese, Abdul. Of course I was thrilled by new sights and new experiences and the fascinations of the Middle East. Clearly this was going to be enjoyable. But what had I been brought there to do? The Bishop had already gone home. So I could not be given any proper briefing and had little idea what was expected of me or exactly in what archdeaconing consisted. That, he had said, can wait till I come back. And in truth there was awfully little that we *could* do. In wintertime everything would have been quite different. But it was unfortunate that I had arrived in the depth of the hot season and the holidays, when the greater part of the English population were on leave, at home or in Cyprus or elsewhere, and most of the Church's activities were closed down. In practice, not very much more was possible than looking after All Saint's cathedral and, between us, taking the services on Sundays. It was not, just then, much more than a holiday chaplaincy. Had the Archbishop, I sadly wondered, been right?

With such few of the English residents as remained, who showed me great kindness, I formed some warm friendships and kept in touch with them for years afterwards. And one of the best fruits of these months was getting to know that great man Temple Gairdner, the CMS secretary in Egypt, a saint and a Christian statesman of the first rank. With him from time to time I went out to the Pyramids and slept the night in the desert under the stars. (The last time I was there, elderly and comfort-loving, we slept luxuriously at the Mena House.)

Egypt was still then under British 'protection', but the tide of nationalism was rising fast and there had been serious riots and demonstrations in which Lord Allenby, at that time Resident, whose predecessor had been murdered, showed great personal courage and resolution. Of course we regarded the nationalists as trouble-makers. The British Empire was still the British Empire and determined to keep control of the Canal. We had little sympathy with 'disloyal elements'. Among Gwynne's endearing limitations were his archaic political opinions. His brother was editor of the *Morning Post*, which he used to call 'that little Christian newspaper'. To the end of his days he took Cromer's word as the final word, a holy scripture from which he never deviated.

I was duly commanded to lunch at the Residency, but His Excellency was so undisguisedly bored with me that he got up from the table and walked out, leaving his wife (who was a parson's daughter and knew what to say) to do her best with me. (Strangely enough, it fell to me years later to bury his ashes in Westminster Abbey.)

I attempted archidiaconal visitations, as Crewe Hamilton told me I should, to some of the outstations in the Delta, and to places like Alexandria and Heliopolis, but with little conception what I was meant to do. How *could* any young man know what to do who had never himself been a parish priest? Perhaps my main contribution to the diocese was that I began to sell the cathedral! It was rather a shabby and shoddy little building, which had been run up by an Army engineer, and was by now quite in the wrong place. The diocese had already decided to demolish it and build something better on a fine site given by the Egyptian Government. I began the negotiations for the sale of it. The magnificent new All Saints' Cathedral standing on the foot of the Kasr-el-Nil Bridge, was afterwards consecrated by William Temple. It must now be rather a white elephant, when there is no Anglican bishop in Egypt, though I think it is used by the Coptic congregations — the oldest Christian communities in existence. But it was amply and more than amply justified when it was thronged by troops of the 8th Army, who flocked to receive Gwynne's ministrations to them.

Egypt gave me the wonderful opportunity of paying my first and only visit to Palestine, then also going through a time of troubles. I went, of course, by train from Kantara. (With the 11th Division in the desert I had ministered to some RE units who were beginning to lay down that railway in preparation for Allenby's campaign, and had ridden out on the first little metre-gauge puff-puff.) In Jerusalem Canon Stacey Waddy, with whom I stayed at St. George's, gave me introduction to the holy places and took me down to Jericho and the Dead Sea. I was able to get time alone to walk and meditate on the Mount of Olives; and the view of the city, at which the Lord wept, seems to be still printed on my retina. I spent a few days at a hostel in Nazareth, then down to the shore — and my heart leapt up, in an exaltation which I can still remember, on seeing the Lake of Galilee with my own eyes. I went up Carmel and finally down to Haifa, and bathed in that ancient river, the river Kishon. That visit is one of my most thankful memories, dimly though I can now recall any details of it. One of our dreams is to go back together. It seems extremely unlikely to be realised.

But I was now informed, to my astonishment, that my teaching application had been taken seriously — partly, no doubt, through the support of Davidson — and that I had been elected by the Council to the Chair of the New Testament at King's College. The Bishop had now come back from leave and stayed a few days on his way up to Khartoum. He had seen the Archbishop at Lambeth and knew about it, and was all magnanimity and understanding. He told me that it was my duty to go; and I know how much he had been looking forward to having me once again under his command. And I too should certainly have learnt much. As it was, I had hardly any opportunity of seeing, or taking any humble share in, the grand old man's work in his vast diocese, and would gladly have stayed with him for a few years. But it was really under obedience that I closed this brief, undistinguished interlude. Though I tried again later to get work overseas, the decree was that I should remain in England.

V

King's College, London

In October, accordingly, I was back in London and assumed my new role as a professor. Among all those experienced and distinguished scholars I must have seemed something like a boy-professor. I cannot conceive how I ever got elected. The electors must have been charitable enough to detect in me some kind of promise — and my record at Knutsford may have helped in that — but it was not, quite certainly, on attainment. I had written nothing in learned periodicals and had published no book on the New Testament, apart from some popular lectures on Ephesians. I knew enough to teach undergraduates; and could hope, by dint of a lot of homework, to maintain a respectable academic standard. But for anything more advanced than that, for any post-graduate teaching or supervision, or for trained research, I was totally unqualified, and could not, by any stretch of imagination, have ranked as a university professor. So I had to try to justify my existence and make such contribution as I was able. My new colleagues gave me a very generous welcome, and the Council kindly assigned me a set of rooms in the King's College hostel in Vincent Square.

The pre-war Church had made few worst mistakes — as I have already remarked in earlier books (*Asking the Right Questions*, and elsewhere) — than in its attempt to segregate ordinands from the sceptical atmosphere of the universities and collect them in safe theological colleges, unless it was its aloof and suspicious attitude towards the new university foundations. Durham was churchy and could just get by. But to most bishops and clergy before the first war names like London or Manchester suggested second-rate and provincial institutions. Besides, the new universities were 'pagan'. They did not acknowledge the queen of sciences. University College, London, was founded in the heyday of Jeremy Bentham's influence, by way of protest against the clerical dominance still prevailing at Oxford and Cambridge. King's, in its turn, was founded as a church college by way of protest against Jeremy Bentham. But in the new universities as a whole Christian theology was not recognised as a proper subject of academic study. Here in London, however, had been the one exception.

Though King's is now one constituent college in the vast corpus of London University, it is a university in itself and will soon be teaching within its walls more students than there were in the whole of pre-war Oxford. It had, as I say, been founded as a church college, and all its early principals had been clerics. But, owing largely, I think, to the foresight — and one might add, the invincible pugnacity — of A. C. Headlam, afterwards Bishop of Gloucester, a far-reaching reorganisation had been carried through not long before the war. What emerged from it was the King's that we know today. In a constitution that sounds immensely complicated, the college was organised under a lay principal with the whole range of academic disciplines, but embracing the Theological Department, which retained a large measure of autonomy, in such a way that the dean of the department was *ex officio* dean of the whole college. Here, then, there was a Faculty of Theology, still largely responsible to the Church, integrated into the constitution of a college which was itself a constituent element in the secular University of London. (The development of the Faculty of Theology to its present influential position in the wider world of London University is hardly within the scope of a personal record.) Headlam had persuaded the bishops — or as some were afterwards to protest, browbeaten them — into recognising the A.K.C. diploma as a degree equivalent for ordinands.

The Principal when I arrived was Ernest Barker, from whom I had imbibed, as an undergraduate, the elements of Greek political theory. This great man, whose friendship I kept till the

PERIOD OF MY LIFE

end, was essentially a Christian humanist. Though he spoke a broad Cheshire Doric, few men I have known seemed to be more at home at once in Athens and in Jerusalem – an authority on the philosophy of politics and the editor of Augustine's *City of God*. He had come to the top the hard way; and his personal memoir, *Father to the Man*, is perhaps the best tribute ever paid to the education of a village school. After a rather unfortunate beginning, he was by now firmly established as an admirable and trusted head of the college. Alike as thinker and teacher and as a Christian, he made himself felt through the whole life of the place. But administration had little real attraction for him and a few years later he left for a chair at Cambridge.

The dean at the time was W. R. Matthews, then at the beginning of a long and eminent career in the Church of England which was to lead to the Deanery of St. Paul's. His outstanding mental ability, his gifts as a teacher and his personal charm permeated the Theological Department. There are many elderly parsons today who count it as one of their most valued privileges to have been at King's in the time of Matthews. My friendship with him has continued ever since.

There were other distinguished members of the teaching staff. Richard Hanson (afterwards dean) taught Philosophy. Hanson had certainly a brilliant mind and had thought much more deeply than most about fundamental theological questions. But he always gave one the impression of being a troubled and rather frustrated man; and, whatever the reason, he never produced the great book which he seemed to have it in him to write. Claude Jenkins, formerly Lambeth librarian and subsequently professor at Oxford, who held the chair of Ecclesiastical History) – was an immensely learned historian and something of an academic 'character', the subject of many imaginative legends. H. M. Relton, a dogmatic theologian, lectured authoritatively on Christology. Clement Rogers, also a bit of an eccentric, taught a great deal of hard commonsense from his chair of Pastoral Theology. The exquisite Percy Dearmer was lecturing in his exquisite clothes on ecclesiastical art. And among my colleagues, towering over them all, there was, by a strange turn of the wheel of fortune, no less a figure than Bishop Gore, who, having resigned the see of Oxford to devote himself to writing his trilogy on *The Reconstruction of Belief*, had been offered a visiting professorship.

The students were, as always, a mixed bag, with ability ranging from a bare pass in the GOE (which had not yet been invented) to decent honours in the Schools or Tripos. They were looking to us to provide them with the equipment for a pastoral and teaching ministry. They had to be introduced to critical scholarship, and never allowed to escape from its rigour by falling back on a literalist biblicism. But it would have been useless to try to turn them into second-rate or third-rate 'scholars'. What they needed was a theology for use. Pure exegesis, therefore, was not enough. They had to understand, first of all, with all the aids scholarship could offer them, what the New Testament writers were saying in their own idiom to their own contemporaries. But the question remained, what are they saying to us in our very different cultural situation? And that meant an attempt at what would now be called the contextualisation of theology. I did my best to exhibit the New Testament not as a textbook of dogmatic formulas but as the mediation of a living faith and always, in my lecturing, with one eye on the contemporary situation. One year when I Corinthians was the set book, we had a wonderful time in trying to think out the place of the Church in a mixed society. Those lectures were quoted to me recently by one who had heard them at the time — something like forty-five years ago.

The teaching load was reasonably heavy. For what we had been doing all day we had to repeat all over again at night. King's was then running an evening course for men who, for financial or other reasons, were precluded from full daytime attendance. They were earning their living during working hours and would then come in (heroic souls!) for lectures for two or three hours before they went home. Moreover, they had to do two calendar years to count for any one academic year.

They were tired, of course, before they started, and to do them any kind of justice the teacher had to make quite exceptional efforts. Some of the ablest men I have ever taught, among them some who have since risen to high office, came up by this gruelling and laborious route.

But the evening classes met a real need; and with five-day weeks and shorter office hours a course of that kind need not now be nearly so burdensome. The need still persists. I am sure that if I were still in office I should seek more and more for the older ordinands, men with some experience of life behind them, and should therefore have to find ways of training them. The scheme sponsored by the Southwark diocese somewhat on the model of sandwich courses, commonly known as 'earn while you learn', seems to have offered the Church a new pattern which has many intrinsic values in itself and can, incidentally, save it a mint of money.

In addition to all these day and evening classes, there was a special department for women — some of whom were very able people and on a higher level than most of the men — preparing to take the Lambeth diploma. This meant getting up a separate course of lectures. But it was a definitely rewarding effort. Only last month I received a letter from one of those who attended these sessions, referring to lectures of mine that she had endured (or as she kindly put it, enjoyed) no less than forty-seven years ago.

Of course I knew best, and was able to do most for, the men assigned to me as personal pupils, and some of these I still number among my friends. The best known of them is Tom Craske, who in the course of his life has been ubiquitous in the activities of the Church of England, to become in the end Bishop of Gibraltar and after that, Moderator of CACTM. Another was Marcus Knight, now Dean of Exeter, living in the house that Matthews built. There were many others now doing important jobs, some of whom had been with me on reading parties, or walked Swiss passes with me in the long vacation; but they might be embarrassed if I were to name them all here.

Some have already crossed the river. Living in the hostel, I was in daily contact with a large proportion of those whom I was teaching, and was able to know many of them intimately. Before long I was appointed sub-warden (the dean being *ex officio* warden) and was thus charged with direct pastoral oversight and responsibility for its internal discipline. In a London hostel the latter was not too easy, and I had to do some very unpopular things. But the men supported me grandly and gave me their trust; and together we made it, I think, a happy community, controlled rather by a free acceptance of certain standards and voluntary principles than by regulations imposed by authority. The hostel was meant for the Theological Faculty. But we did not want our ordinands segregated; and during my time a certain number of men from other departments of the college joined us as residents in Vincent Square — I hope to their own advantage, but indubitably to the great advantage of the theologians.

Outside King's I had many other activities. Mervyn Haigh was chaplain at Lambeth and during these years we were in constant touch. We would walk at Richmond on Saturday afternoons and from time to time took holidays together. We were able in endless talk to look further down some of those new theological trails which we had begun to explore at Knutsford; and I well remember a moment on Lulworth Downs when I first began to see that 'the Christian ethic' cannot be derived simply from direct quotation from the Gospels (or 'applying the Sermon on the Mount'), but that the actual content of the Christian life must always be variable and contextual.

A characteristic remark of Randall Davidson's deepened and reinforced that understanding. Younger clergy are always in revolt against the stuffiness of the institution, and ill would it be for the Church if they were not. Our generation were mesmerised by St. Francis, whom we tended to quote as the one real Christian, and were always clamouring to high authority to franciscanise the Church of England. I was often in Mervyn's room at Lambeth and now and again was invited into the study. One day the Archbishop led me to his bookshelves and put in my hands one of Coulton's books. "Read that," he said, "and try to make up your mind what you think St. Francis would have done had he been, not a layman in the twelfth century, but Archbishop of Canterbury in the twentieth. When you know the answer, come back and tell me." I returned the book, but I do not yet know the answer. Of course it was a veiled form of the question, What does loyalty to the spirit of Christ demand of us in our world, so different from his, in situations which he did not foresee and for which he was not laying down legislation? There can surely be no *a priori* answer. (I should not, however, wish to be understood as endorsing 'situation ethics'.)

During these years I was still in contact with a good many of the rebel groups which revolved, at various distances, round Dick Sheppard; and was closely involved with Mervyn, Leslie Hunter, Harold Anson, Dwelly, Dearmer and others, in compiling and publishing the Grey Book — a liberal proposal for a revised Prayer Book, to which William Temple wrote the preface. The bishops do not seem to have bothered to look at it; they might have produced a better book if they had. In particular, they might have attempted what still very urgently needs doing — a revision of the Collects, Epistles and Gospels. Even today, the chatty little rites provided by the Liturgical Commission as alternatives to Cranmer's liturgy, still leave the worshipper at Holy Communion with too many unintelligible epistles from St. Paul's more donnish speculations. ('Agar is Mount Sinai in Arabia'; 'to Abraham and his seed were the promises made'; etc.)[1] The actual procedure by which the bishops went to work on the revision has been described in my *Mervyn Haigh*, pp. 85–9; and all the time they were asking the wrong question — not how to worship God in the twentieth

[1] Since this was written, the Commission has published a new Eucharistic lectionary, proposing a revision of Collects, Epistles and Gospels, framed in a drastically rearranged Calendar. I have not had opportunity to study it.

century, but how to restore liturgical discipline, a thing which can only be done by consent and can never be imposed from the top.

It is only formally true to say that Parliament rejected the so-called Deposited Book. It was really wrecked, like other schemes since then, by a coalition of the two extremes within the Church of England itself. The result seemed like the end of the world at the time. Perhaps it was really a merciful deliverance.

The General Strike occurred while I was at King's. I took part at night with some of the students in helping to unload milk at Waterloo, destined (or so we were told) for sick children. I am less sure now whether it was not strike-breaking. More importantly, I recall being taken by the Archbishop through the unlighted streets to address a meeting that he had called in Queen's Hall. The BBC had refused him leave to broadcast. But the intervention of the Churches made a deep impression on the workers and Davidson was cheered in the streets — an infrequent experience for Archbishops. Shortly afterwards he invited me to lecture to his clergy school at Canterbury and I had the immense privilege of staying with him and Mrs. Davidson in the Old Palace and learning more of the mind of that great old man — whom Gore called 'the wisest man in all England'. At this time, too, I was in close touch with Garbett, then in his redoubtable Southwark period, and as one of his examining chaplains was fairly often at Bishop's House, Kennington, and present at nearly all his ordinations.

I was a junior member, indeed the baby, of the Archbishops' Doctrinal Commission, which was formed originally (1922) to investigate what varieties of interpretation could be comprehended within the Church of England, at once catholic, reformed and 'broad', with a special view to Eucharistic doctrine, radical divergences about which threatened to tear the Church in half, and later wrecked the 1927 Prayer Book. But it vastly widened the scope of its discussion and did not report till 1938. By that time the whole situation had changed and the questions that were being asked were different questions. The findings were dated already before they were published. Yet the report is still well worth reading, and if anyone reads it today he might be surprised to discover how 'liberal' it was, and what a width of interpretation it allowed as legitimate in the Church of England. Thus it has still a contemporary relevance. Dr. Matthews, Sir Walter Moberly and myself are, I think, the only survivors of what was then a company of young men. (For Dr. Matthews' own impression, see his *Memories and Meanings* (Hodder and Stoughton), pp. 143 ff.)

These years, then, were years of widening interests, and they were, I hope, years of growth. But I still wanted to work overseas, and was glad to be offered several opportunities of Christian educational posts abroad. But either the doctor rejected me for the tropics or for other reasons all of them fell through; and finally my friend Garfield Williams, who was then running the Missionary Council (and was subsequently Dean of Manchester) told me that I must make up my mind that I was 'meant' to stay put in England. After I had been some years at King's, Trinity College invited me, out of the blue, to go to Cambridge as Vicar of Great St. Mary's. I consulted two intimate friends at Cambridge – Edward Woods, still vicar of Holy Trinity, and B. K. Cunningham of Westcott House – and both, to my surprise, were uncompromising in advising me not to touch it at any price. They said, "You will only break your heart for no good; there is nothing whatever that anybody can do with it." Since then, a Stockwood, a Fison, a Montefiore have disproved those gloomy prognostications. As it turned out, I went instead to Oxford, to a task that seemed hardly less impossible.

For there soon happened to me something that cannot have happened to many other people. In a single week I received the offer both of Portsea and of St. Mary's, Oxford. There was only one man who had held both these posts and that was the Archbishop of York. So I sought his help, and without hesitation he told me that Oxford was the right answer. I was now involved in a schizophrenic tension between two opposed fields of force – Garbett (who must, I suppose, have put my name forward) throwing all his weight in favour of Portsea, Lang with archiepiscopal authority almost ordering me to accept St. Mary's. Archbishop Davidson was no less emphatic. And of course the two Archbishops were perfectly right. If I had gone to Portsea at that stage the result would have been a humiliating failure for myself and disaster for the parish. I had no parochial experience at all. How *could* I have been the leader of all those curates?

Oxford, therefore, it clearly had to be. But it was not so simple as it sounded. Ever since Newman's day, and indeed before that, the vicarage of the university Church has always been held in conjunction with a fellowship. Without that, the living which Oriel was offering me had an income of £116 — though the college proposed to add another £100 — and the vicar would have to provide his own housing. This seemed to be totally impracticable. But a letter then arrived from the Master of Balliol asking whether I would feel disposed to join his college as fellow and chaplain, undertaking some part-time tutorial work. By his arrangement I had a long conversation with him at some wayside station — I cannot remember where — and told him at once that of course, at least on Sundays, I should not be able to take chapel services; so how could I serve the college as chaplain? Other provisions, he said, could be made for that: they wanted a pastor rather than a service-taker. He then asked me whether I should feel able, in addition to taking pupils in Theology (which I felt I could conscientiously attempt) to give help with men in their first year of Greats. As to that I was bound to feel extremely diffident; my Plato and Aristotle were so rusty. But I could only say that, if the College thought fit to make a definite offer, I should feel it an honour to accept. The sequel belongs to the next chapter. But I can never be grateful enough to Balliol for receiving me into that distinguished Common Room on conditions so advantageous to me, so little advantageous to them.

So this period of my life was closing. The men gave me a wonderful send-off and carried me round the hostel shoulder high. Two years later, the Council did me the honour of electing me as a fellow of King's College.

VI

Oxford revisited

NO ONE, PERHAPS, could be vicar of St. Mary's without being
conscious of the ghost of Newman; and least of all if he had
been brought up, as I had been, in Newman's own college. I
had rooms on his staircase as an undergraduate, as a fellow I
lived with the portraits and the legends, and now I was to
inherit his pulpit. Like him, I had hoped and expected nothing
else than 'to live and die as a fellow of Oriel'. As I have related,
things worked out differently, and for the last twelve years I
had been working in France or in Cheshire or in London.
Now I was back, as fellow of a great college very different in
ethos and tradition, and in a recognisably different Oxford,
which, though it was still pre-revolutionary — pre-Hitler,
pre-Hiroshima, pre-Einstein and pre-Professor Ayer — was no
longer that of the pre-war summer term. It was, as was said 'getting back to normal'. The ex-brigadiers and sergeant-majors who
had filled it after the war were mostly gone now, to give place
to boys coming straight from school. They had not been through
that experience, but their fathers and elder brothers had —
and many of these had been killed in the war — and this
could hardly have failed to make its mark on themselves
and on what they made of Oxford. It was not the same closed
world that it had been. The undergraduates seemed to be quite
as carefree — they could not know that *their* world was so soon to
end; but there was, I should say, a far more open climate of
social and political awareness. The Angry Young Man had
not yet made his appearance. Student protest was something
still in the future. In his *Party Games* Christopher Mayhew has
described the middle-class socialism and communism of the

Oxford he left a few years later than this. "We were wrong", he says, "but let no-one say we were wrong in a mean or selfish manner." He goes on to point out a significant contrast. "The student extremists of my generation were intelligent and articulate, expounding their ideas coherently in speeches, articles and books. They did not simply shout slogans in the streets. Some of them also had courage; they fought against Mosley's uniformed Blackshirts, against armed Fascists in Spain, and eventually some of them against Germany. They did not confine their attacks to unarmed London policemen." Describing a debate in the Union in 1968, and the behaviour of Mr. Tariq Ali and his supporters, Mr. Mayhew remarks that "as their applause and heckling began, they seemed to be even more self-righteous, dogmatic and partisan. Their passion seemed more personal, more immediate, than ours, springing more from temperament and less from intellectual conviction. . . . This alternative to rational argument seems to me to sum up the decline in student extremism since the thirties."[1]

But the war had shaken the old unquestioning certainties, and not only the social and political certainties, but also the moral and religious. One sign of that was the end of 'compulsory chapel'. Under pressure from the ex-service generation the colleges may have surrendered too lightly something that can now never be recovered – the whole principle of corporate worship as an integral part of the life of their communities. As

[1] The *Sunday Times*, 17th August 1969. Dr. James Parkes, as one of "the generation which witnessed the great divide between pre-1914 satisfaction and the worth-while but lost battle of the post-war years", gives a very interesting impression of the difference in student attitudes after the first war and after the second. At the SCM conference in Glasgow (1921) "we could find and talk to men and women who could speak from experience on the problems of all the continents and on almost every career which offered opportunities of Christian service. It is a measure of the significant change after the second world war that at the Westminster quadrennial of 1947 the students wanted only to hear each other talk, and to discuss on a level we would have found inadequate in a study circle of freshmen." (*Voyage of Discoveries*, Gollancz, 1969, pp. 248, 58.) I reproduce this without comment, but the whole discussion there is a valuable social document.

always in times of social change there were already latent the seeds of new theologies and new moralities: Why shouldn't I? was the all-pervading question. It was plain to see that traditional Christianity was already beginning to count for much less in the life of the university than previously and tending to become a marginal interest. Could it be got back into the centre again? That was the problem posed for me by St. Mary's.

Whatever might be the answer to that, a perfectly tangible job was under my hands in what I had undertaken to do at Balliol. The college of my adoption received me with a warm-hearted and encouraging friendliness. It was what is now referred to as Lindsay's Balliol; and although there were certain quickly discerned tensions – for the Master had strong views of his own which were not by any means always those of Jowett – it was a gay and stimulating society. Some of the classical figures were still there – the half-legendary F. F. Urquhart, the (to me) rather alarming Pickard-Cambridge, Harold Hartley (still vigorous in his nineties), Kenneth Bell, and Cyril Bailey, married to Creighton's daughter, an eminent authority on Lucretius and a man with a genius for friendship who gave me unsparing help in all manner of ways. Most of these will be little more than names to any who may be reading this now, but they were great men in their day and generation.

A. D. Lindsay (Sandy), I met for the first time at the interview recorded in the last chapter. But, from now on, the better I got to know him the greater became my affection and respect. As a son of Principal Lindsay of Glasgow he was a dyed-in-the-wool Church of Scotland man, but we worked together in perfect understanding. His judgement may not always have been infallible; he may have spread himself a bit too widely; he may have tried to impose on his college a pattern to which it was resistant; and no doubt his political views were provocative – or at least they were in the Oxford of that period. Anyone who wanted to could make criticisms (but who is there of whom that is not true?). But he was, all the same, a great man and a great Christian. In after years he stayed with us at Southwell and more than once we visited him and his wife in their vacation cottage in Eskdale. When he became Lord Lindsay of Birker I met him from time to time in the House of Lords; but when he died I was in America and could not even be present at his funeral. The Keele of his own vision is his memorial.

Of the men, more or less of my own age, in the Common Room, the classical tutors were a brilliant group, all of them predictably on their way to the top. There was John Macmurray, afterwards Professor, whose Gifford Lectures, *The Form of the Personal*, have set metaphysics, I hope and believe, on a new track. There was (Sir) Roger Mynors, who seemed to have incarnated in himself the ideal of 'humane letters', now Professor of Latin at Oxford; and two future Vice-chancellors and public figures, Charles Morris and John Fulton, both now noble lords.

There was, too, at this time in other colleges, a vintage of singularly gifted younger dons, all of whom admitted me to their friendship, who were to rise to prominent positions in the educational world or in public life. I might mention here, for example, John Christie, Headmaster of Repton and Westminster and Principal of Jesus College, Oxford; Oliver (Lord) Franks, Ambassador at Washington; and John (Lord Redcliffe) Maud, Secretary of the Ministry of Education, Master of Birkbeck, High Commissioner in South Africa, Master of University College and author, amongst other things, of the Maud Report. Richard Crossman was a young don at New College. (The Crosland, Jenkins, Harold Wilson troika had not yet come up as undergraduates, nor was Edward Heath yet at Balliol.)

These men and others like them were for me proofs of the old Oxford claim, now derided as hopelessly amateurish, that a trained mind and a liberal education will equip men to do the practical jobs. The Civil Service was built on that belief. In our time, universities were regarded as places of liberal education, which is not to say that they could not be also vocational;

the mediaeval schools were vocational, but within an acknowledged value-system and in relation to a cultural whole. They were not just high-power factories for technicians. A man, after all, is more than his techniques, and if that is not recognised in his education, then he is being expensively dehumanised. I suspect that much of the student unrest today is due to a dawning awareness of that and resentment at the idea of being moulded as spare parts of a technical society, the ruling values of which they repudiate, rather than being helped to fulfil their humanness.

With the junior undergraduates living in college, I began pretty soon to establish relations and am still in touch with some of the friends I made then, in their sedate and distinguished occupations. I was bidden to preach sometimes in the college chapel. I did my best with the teaching work assigned to me and initiated a couple of years of Greats men into their reading of Plato and Aristotle. There were also a few, very few, Theological pupils. But one could do justice to all this only by concentrating one's whole time and thought on it, and this was meant to be only a part-time job. There was still St. Mary's and what could be done with *that*?

When the bishop (Tommy Strong) came to institute me he had been, as always, thoroughly realistic, and made clear that he had no illusions about the low estate of St. Mary's. When I made the declaration against Simony in the vestry beforehand he remarked, quite audibly, "If you had paid anything for *this*, I should call it drawing iniquity with a cartrope". But he had put himself to immense trouble. He threw a party at Oriel after the service, and invited a number of dons and undergraduates, doing everything within his power to make it a university occasion. It did not feel at all like that at the time. St. Mary's is one of the ancient city parishes and the vicar owes his existence to his benefice. The parish comprises All Souls and Brasenose, the St. Mary Hall quadrangle of Oriel and a few shops in the High and King Edward Street. If one leaves out the colleges in term time, the population might have been about a hundred; and to that minute cure I was officially instituted. The two parish churchwardens, I remember, rejoiced in the names of Messrs. Ham and Smallbone—which seemed to me at the time to be symbolic of the half-pathetic, half-comic situation. But the Vice-chairman of the PCC was C. H. Sampson ('Sammy'), Principal of Brasenose, a keen and meticulously-minded churchman, eager to show me the way in which I should go. After almost every service a note arrived in his totally illegible handwriting pointing out what I had done that I ought not to have done and what I had left undone that I ought to have done. But in all that followed he was a tower of strength to me. Two or three women, headed by Hilda Jenkinson, wife of the philosopher, A. J. Jenkinson (who was shortly afterwards killed in a mountain accident), did such sparse good works as the parish needed. That seemed to be all; that was what I had to work upon.

But that was my primary responsibility. There were three parish services every Sunday, though one would have been amply sufficient. I took a great deal of trouble with the sermons — had not some of Newman's finest efforts been published as 'parochial' sermons? — and tried to make the worship as 'real' as possible. Soon the tiny handful began to grow. We were joined, for example, by the extremely gifted and formidable Mrs. Mandell Creighton, then living close to her daughter, Mrs. Bailey. (When I once went to visit her in her sickroom she greeted me by saying, "Young man, I don't believe you know what to do." It was only too true, but I hoped that I had concealed the facts.) Dons' wives and families started to come from north Oxford, which in those days stopped quite a way short of Banbury. Slowly and gradually there was built up a rather eclectic morning congregation, alive, responsive and anxious to be given some intelligible and credible theology. The evening congregations were still pitiful.

But St. Mary's was also the university church, indeed the earliest home of the university, standing there at the centre of the colleges, with its spire dominating the Oxford skyline,

95

witnessing in stone to what they had meant by *Dominus illumina-tio mea*. Was it now no more than one of the lost enchantments? Was its function merely to be an auditorium for thinly attended university sermons? For, as I was to learn in Nottingham, a church standing empty on a strategic site may be doing a lot of positive harm, seeming to witness to gods that have failed. So far as related to the university, St. Mary's seemed to be making the admission that what had been at the centre of its life was no longer of public or communal importance – and that, according to Dr. Bryan Wilson, is what secularisation means. Could the church become once again a central power-station making itself felt in the life and thought of Oxford?

I did not believe then, any more than I believe now, that the primary aim of Christianity, or of the clergy, is simply to fill churches. You can fill churches by cheapening what is offered in them; but what Christian ends have been served by that? Yet I felt that if St. Mary's could once again be crowded with undergraduates week by week, that would be an important act of witness which could do what at that time most needed doing, and put Christianity back on the map of Oxford. I decided to try to revive the evening sermons, which had fallen into abeyance since the war years. A tentative start was made almost at once but the audience were at first mainly townspeople – good in itself but not what I was out for. Towards the end of my second year, however, a great piece of good fortune came to me. Harry Baines, who had gone down from Balliol a year or so before I arrived and had since been working for the Student Christian Movement, had now finished his preparation at Cuddesdon, and agreed to come to St. Mary's as curate, combining that with the part-time secretaryship of the Oxford branch of the SCM. This meant an enormous access of power, not only because of what he himself brought to us but because the church and the movement were drawn into partnership in his own person. Thus began a close and intimate friendship which has lasted through all the stages of his career. He is now Bishop of Wellington, New Zealand.

From that moment things began to happen. The SCM made itself responsible for supporting the evening sermons in St. Mary's — though I reserved the right to choose the preachers — and gave me the most splendid co-operation. Among the first and doughtiest undergraduate helpers I recall three who are now diocesan bishops — Cyril Easthaugh, Cuthbert Bardsley and Gerald Ellison. What was to consolidate this experiment was, of course, the famous mission of William Temple, which had been planned before my arrival by a committee under C. S. Emden, then Principal of St. Edmund Hall, with whom I was brought into close and valued contact, and for which I had now to assume responsibility. But before it happened there were two big events, one of public and one of private interest, which I must record before going on to the mission.

The first is the restoration of the church. It had been discovered soon after I took over that the depredations of the familiar beetle had virtually destroyed the roof timbers as well as some of the beams in the tower, leaving the structure in danger of collapse and necessitating some very expensive works. They must be put in hand and without delay. So we were in for a big fund-raising effort. But here was a chance too good to be missed. If we were going to spend all that money, why should we not attempt at the same time to do something more radical and imaginative, to take out the hideous clutter of galleries which had been introduced in the eighteenth century, and uncover the church in its grand scale and proportions as the original builders had designed it? So I got together a powerful committee to advise and help me in working out such a scheme and to shoulder the task of finding means to finance it. Sir Charles Nicholson was asked to make plans to show us what the result would be and, after many meetings and consultations, the committee decided to go ahead. With clerical help from a large number of people we prepared to issue a nation-wide appeal, which was to include among its professed objects a capital sum towards endowing the benefice.

But "You can't do that there 'ere" as the policeman said.

"Not in Oxford, you can't," he might have added. As St. Mary's was the university church there had to be long, solemn correspondence with organs of university authority. And as soon as the project began to get about there arose an un-believable storm of protest. Oriel, as patron, opposed the scheme. There were resolutions, letters in the press, broadsheets addressed to members of Congregation – all the apparatus of academic controversy. The opposition was led by Sir Michael Sadler, Master of University, on the ground that St. Mary's must now and forever remain what it had been when Newman preached in it. Later on, when the work was actually in progress. someone persuaded him to go and look at it. He went, he saw and surrendered unconditionally, and wrote me a generous letter of retractation. After that St. Mary's had a few more devoted friends.

The storm took years to blow itself out. But when it seemed to have died down sufficiently to make it safe to venture out of harbour, we put in our application for a faculty and com-missioned Sir Charles to make a start. The result was what Oxford sees today – and assumes, maybe, that it was never otherwise! He removed the enormous projecting gallery which had covered the whole of the north side of the nave, jutting out a long way over the floor, thus opening up the north aisle and its chapels to reveal the magnificent mediaeval church in its earlier glory as a place of worship. At the same time the chancel was opened up to the nave. (The figures in the niches above the high altar were replaced by a gift from the Church Union to mark the centenary of the Tractarian Movement.) In this sense, if no other, I left my mark on St. Mary's; a boss in the roof of the north aisle depicts a chalice labelled with my initials. In the forty years and more that have passed since, many other improvements have been made. It must be thirty since I was last invited there. But when I visited it as a tripper lately I felt that, however much I had failed in other ways, at least I had given Oxford back its great church.

The other event, which came so unexpectedly like a blessing

out of the sky, was my marriage. This was to change my whole personal life; and it is to St. Mary's that I owe it. The 'girl from Girton' at Holy Trinity Cambridge was the daughter of George Buchanan Gray, Old Testament Professor at Mansfield College. He had died suddenly some years before this—so that I have never known my wife's father—but his widow had stayed on in Oxford with her two children. Her daughter, after coming down from Cambridge, was secretary to H. A. L. Fisher, and in fact typed the *History of Europe*. She had been moved to join the Church of England and had been prepared for confirmation by the Vicar of St. Andrew's, Paul de Labilliere, who was soon to become Bishop of Knaresborough and, later, beloved war-time Dean of Westminster. I had been introduced to Lilian in connexion with some missionary enterprises undertaken by Oxford undergraduates for which she was acting as organising secretary; and when I needed help with my correspondence she accepted my invitation to work with me, and came to my rooms in Balliol every morning. I was in an extremely vulnerable position and in a few months the inevitable happened—it had been freely predicted before it did happen! We became engaged on the Downs above Wantage, which have ever since been rather a sacred place for us. Of all the good gifts that life has given me this has been incomparably the best.

As I am thirteen years older than Lilian we decided not to defer the wedding beyond the end of the coming Michaelmas term. We had the good luck to find a tiny house, tiny, that is, by pre-war standards, with a walled garden behind it, at 12 Holywell, and, though neither of us had any money, set about all the excitements of furnishing.

Like most other people, we were defeated in the hope of a quiet, village-church wedding, and it had to be very publicly, at St. Mary's. After I had published the banns myself—getting the words wrong in my embarrassment—we were married, in front of a packed congregation, on 10th December, 1929. Just as I was leaving for the church there arrived at my rooms a representative of the Ecclesiastical Insurance Office, about something or other to do with my life policy. I apologised and said there was hardly time now, I was being married in less than half an hour. The Ecclesiastical Insurance Office quoted that at me for years after. A galaxy of clergy took part in the service — my father, who did the actual deed, Cyril Garbett, then still at Southwark, Bishop Shaw, Suffragan of Oxford, Paul de Labilliere and several others, for whom it was hard to find anything to do. Mervyn Haigh acted as my best man, and Harry Baines functioned as a most efficient and decorative master of ceremonies. The reception afterwards was in the Hall at Oriel.

For the honeymoon, my friend Owen Hugh Smith, Chairman of Hay's Wharf and later a lay canon of Southwark Cathedral, had lent us his fishing cottage at Hurstbourne Priors. When we went back, I had somehow lost the latch key, and our first entry into our new home was by climbing in through the window in the early hours of the morning.

Marriage interdenominationalised us. For although Lilian had been for some years an Anglican, her mother and some other members of her family were Congregationalists. Through them I came to be accepted as a kind of Congregationalist-in-law. I have been allowed to number some of the leading figures in that Church among my personal friends, and to feel a close attachment to Mansfield, where that great little man W. B. Selbie advised and supported me in many difficulties.

Now that at last I had a home of my own and a place in which people could be seen and welcomed I was in a much stronger pastoral position; and not least in relation to the women's colleges. (I was a kind of unofficial chaplain to Lady Margaret Hall, of which at this time that wonderful woman Lynda Grier was principal, and dedicated Scott's fine new chapel for them.) We did our best, with the small income available, to make our home a centre for undergraduates, keeping open house one evening a week in term time — the house being normally packed to capacity. We also tried to entertain visiting preachers. Our most eminent guest was William Temple, by then Archbishop of York, who stayed with us for the ten days of his mission. To have entertained Lang for one day, or Dean Inge even for one meal, might have involved us both in a nervous breakdown. (In the case of Dean Inge, it very nearly did: he was a most pernickety kind of guest.) To have William with us was pure delight, and for part of the time Mrs. Temple joined us. That week is among our happiest memories. Incidentally, it gave me the chance of watching at close quarters how what he did was done.

Much has been written by myself and others about that now famous mission. He was at his best and most characteristic. The fact that he was now Archbishop of York had given it in advance an inflated news value: Oxford was full of reporters and press photographers. And it may have induced more people to come. But what mattered was that having once come they stayed. The congregations increased night by night; people were sitting on the floor, on the altar steps, anywhere they could be crammed in. But there was no emotional excitement. No psychological pressures were applied. Nothing could have been less like a Billy Graham meeting. At a similar mission — by Gore — in the pre-war period Arthur Burroughs proposed to produce a group of clergy who would walk about the church after the service among broken-hearted and penitent undergraduates, tap them on the shoulder and offer them consolation. "I am profoundly convinced," Gore retorted, "that there must be no accosting. There must certainly be no accosting." (He kept on repeating it, pronounced accorsting.) The popular press was disappointed this time. "Nothing is happening," one of the reporters protested to me! There were no sensations, no sobbing undergraduates, nobody being visibly 'converted'. William spoke quietly and with hardly a gesture. He gave an unemotional presentation, derived from his own Christian experience, and supported by deeply thought rational argument, of the faith which he believed to be true; followed always by an appeal to face it and ask ourselves what this could imply for us. His opening words were "In the beginning, God." Would anyone dare, speaking to such an audience, to begin an argument quite like that today? And would he connect with his hearers if he did? Temple could still count on a friendly philosophy. In that rather disillusioned post-war atmosphere what was lacking was the will to believe. Organised Humanist opposition to the Christian world-view had not yet appeared, though Marxism had its perfervid followers. (A study group met in my room a year or two after this, led by a very able and, at that time, truculent young Marxian named John Strachey.) A detached, sceptical attitude was the fashion, and the young are conformist in their nonconformity. Temple stemmed the tide of conformist irreligion and put religion back on the Oxford map by making it intellectually respectable to profess belief in Christianity; and that was indeed the achievement of his whole life. There are men and women all over the world still who date from those addresses in St. Mary's (afterwards published as *Christian Faith and Life*) their own personal Christian commitment.

His Anglican assistant in the mission was Tom Pym, one of the most brilliant and best-beloved of the wartime chaplains and potentially one of our great post-war leaders, whose life was to be so tragically foreshortened. His addresses on the techniques of prayer and his private conversations with many enquirers perfectly complemented the Archbishop's work.

The Mission addresses were given without notes. They were taken down by a stenographer, for eventual printing in the *Church Times*. She brought me the typescript every morning — a piece of flawless English prose, in which all the sentences were grammatical and even the punctuation seemed to have been spoken. Hardly ever a word needed changing. They were printed almost exactly as they were spoken. The articles were collected in book-form and again very nearly without correction. At its lowest, it was a masterly performance which any experienced speaker might envy. But when or how had all this been prepared? He seemed to think little about it at the time. He would go out after breakfast every morning and be occupied all day with interviews and, for all I know, with his piles of correspondence and only came back to Holywell in the evening. Then we gave him a meal by himself, as a chance to be quiet and concentrate his thoughts. But what he asked for at that point was a thriller. (He had a wide erudition in whodunits.) "The great thing," he said, "is to keep your mind *off* it." I asked him then how he ever did prepare all his innumerable and weighty utterances. He told me that when he booked an engagement he would spend a few minutes making up his mind what line he intended to take at the critical moment. Then he handed it over to his subconscious. When he got to the church the sermon had written itself. This remarkable gift of dissociation was inherited, he once explained, from his father, who could repeat in a sermon, without knowing it, page after page of a book that he had read just once, perhaps many years before. This gift, which I think he took trouble to develop, certainly stood William in good stead in supporting the unending burden of chairmanship. Sometimes he would seem to be paying little attention, writing letters or even nearly asleep. Then, at the end, he would offer a lucid summary of what had been said and the arguments on both sides in a lengthy and intricate discussion. This became astonishingly apparent in his chairmanship of the Doctrinal Commission.

The mission, of course, gave an immense impetus to what Harry and I were trying to do at St. Mary's. The evening sermons were now firmly established and continued to draw crowded congregations. The most eminent preachers were glad to be invited and some rather offended if they were not. The sermons were planned to make continuous courses, and invited preachers had to be carefully briefed so as to fit in with one another; which involved a good deal of thought and letter-writing. I remember one course which might have been planned today, advertised as 'Science without morals, Morals without religion, Religion without God'. We were not altogether blind to the signs of the times. Each term I took two or three of the sermons myself; and I have since met people all over the world with whom these had given me personal contact. Some years ago I was taken to visit a grammar school way out in Uganda. The headmaster greeted me with the words, "Last time I saw you was in St. Mary's pulpit."

Through St. Mary's also I was drawn into close touch with the Student Christian Movement world, its leaders like Tissington Tatlow and Hugh Martin, and their clientele in the various universities. There must be few pre-Robbins universities in which I have not preached or given addresses. And, failing William Temple or Reinhold Niebuhr, who was at that time one of the student idols — 'Thou shalt love thy Niebuhr as thyself' — I was constantly in demand at student conferences. Indeed at one time, had I wished or been able to, I might have spent most of my life at Swanwick. There I frequently met Fr. Herbert Kelly, who exercised so profound an influence on that whole generation of students, and to whom my own subsequent thinking owes so much. Through him, though at the time we were not aware of it, some of us were first introduced to the theology of F. D. Maurice, whose disciple he always claimed to be.

All these activities meant more personal contacts. And what between Knutsford, King's College and St. Mary's, I have known a considerable proportion of the Anglican clergy, including some of the bishops, during their undergraduate phases. This was to give me, when I became more senior, a kind of quasi-patriarchal status.

Fairly early during our time at Oxford I was appointed a chaplain to the King (George V), a post which I held through the two subsequent reigns till I had to relinquish it when I became a bishop. Thus I have enjoyed the privilege of contact not only with George V and Queen Mary, but also with Edward, both as Prince and King, with George VI and the present Queen Mother (who with her amazing royal memory recognised me the other day at a crowded function) and, before her accession, with the present Sovereign. Of this I cherish many delightful memories, of which, however, one does not speak in public. I was also appointed at more or less the same time as a canon theologian of Liverpool. This meant enjoyable visits to preach there and the hospitality of the Dean – that lovable, fascinating, wayward genius, Fred Dwelly.

It was during my tenure of St. Mary's that Buchmanism, calling itself – as we thought at the time rather disingenuously – the Oxford Group, first invaded England. It caused us deep anxiety and perplexity. With all the American apparatus of advertising, the use of big names and lavish expenditure, the Group quickly got the publicity which it sought and without which it could not live. Too soon it became acutely controversial, separating Christians from one another. From some it drew an intense, uncritical loyalty, from others an equally intense repugnance. Grensted lent the authority of his name to it, others with no less right to be heard denounced it. When Lindsay and I issued a statement defending the Group against malicious charges of sexual immorality and so forth, the Balliol Common Room nearly exploded around us. Men and girls whom we knew 'went groupy'; some of them, it seemed, were spiritually re-made, some were brought to the edge of mental breakdown throught the Group's claim to control other people's lives and its unskilled interference in their love affairs.

Neither as vicar nor as college chaplain could I possibly have remained an aloof spectator and not attempted to understand this movement or reach some balanced Christian judgement about it. In this I was greatly helped all the time by the wisdom and insight of Dr. Selbie. I attempted, at the request of the editor, to produce for the *Spectator* a judicious and objective estimate of this neo-Montanism (written during our holiday on a wet day in a primitive *gasthof* in Tirol) to which Henson often referred in flattering terms.[1] Perhaps it was Temple who said the wisest thing: that the best which could happen to a young

[1] The Hensonian reaction to Buchmanism is recorded in his *Retrospect of an Unimportant Life*, II, xxii.

man was to fall into it during his first year and move safely out of it during his second. The initial excitement died down after a while.

In one of the Oxford long vacations we paid our first visit to the United States, the American YMCA having invited me to give some talks to student vacation conferences. We were based on the Union theological seminary, home of so many famous Christian leaders, hard by the Riverside church in New York. I lectured in their vacation courses and gave some addresses in the chapel. Though Manhattan in August is no health resort, this was an enlarging experience – my first contact with the American thought-world; and it gave me the friend-ship, kept up till his death, of that great ecumenist Henry Sloane Coffin, the President. After some engagements on the Eastern seaboard we were sent down into South Carolina, its mountains ablaze with flame-coloured wild azalea, where there were meetings with various groups of students who, to my surprise – it was nearly forty years ago – could not understand what I meant by 'God'. Then back to New York, where on our last evening we were taken to what was then the rage, *Green Pastures*. Before going home we took a short holiday among the lakes across the Canadian border, and were back in Oxford in time for Michaelmas term.

The talks in America crystallised the form of a book on which I had been at work for many years in close consultation with Mervyn Haigh. I began to write it out on the return voyage, Lilian typing the copy as it was written, and worked on it intensively during the next few months. It was published in 1931 as *The Relevance of Christianity*, the title being Lilian's inspiration. This was very warmly received and quickly ran through a number of editions. It was, in a sense, the book that made my name. People still talk to me about 'your book', as though one had never written anything since. But none of my too many later publications has had anything like the same success, though *Christian Ethics and Secular Society*, written and published after my retirement, was, in my own judgement, a better book, more mature and based on far more reading and a wider experience of life — or had the prophetic fire began to die down? But the first was by an up-and-coming young man, and perhaps one can never quite recapture the first, fine careless rapture. Many men have told me since that it was that book which, in the general post-war confusion, made it possible for them to become ordained. A few copies are still sold year by year. Through that book 'relevance' became a catchword.

But work breeds work; and the manifold activities centred on or flowing out from St. Mary's, in addition to my duties in college, soon threatened to produce a log-jam; and most of this time, partly to earn money, I was writing leaders and articles for the (Church) *Guardian*.

It was not, of course, that we did not have holidays. For us these were the highlights of the year. It has always been our principle and practice to cut down on the necessities of life in order to enjoy some modest amenities. Hard-up though we were, we always managed an annual trip to the continent — travelling hard by the old third class with a bag of air cushions from Woolworth's — to the Alps or Maggiore or Como, before package tours had turned them into Butlin's; and these are among the most cherished memories.

But it was becoming increasingly clear to us that the burden of work had somehow got to be lightened. Balliol treated me with extreme generosity, letting me off one thing after another, till at last I was doing almost nothing for them. This seemed to me morally very hard to justify. Could I go on taking their stipend and giving them nothing in return? I felt bound to tell them, as a matter of honour, that I had no choice now but to resign my fellowship, and with it, of course, a large slice of our income. This carried with it the corollary that before long we should have to leave St. Mary's. The Master proposed a different solution, to give up St. Mary's and stay with Balliol. The college offered me a wholetime fellowship, with little teaching, in order to write another book. But I have never been able to write except in a context of pastoral work and against a background of trying to *do* things; and I felt in my bones that, with all its attractions and its flattering implications, this was not for me. So I let this too-good-to-be-true offer go and decided to wait for some post in the Church elsewhere.

This got about, and we were soon bombarded with plausible and implausible suggestions from bishops and others in many different dioceses. But after a while I learnt by the grapevine that a Westminster canonry would soon be vacant and that my name was under consideration for it. I had little doubt that, if that should happen, it would be the almost ideally right solution. In due course a letter came from Ramsay MacDonald offering me the canonry of Westminster annexed to the Rectory of St. John's, Smith Square.

So that was the end of my seven years at St. Mary's. I have but rarely set foot in Oxford since; nowhere is a man so soon forgotten. But I sometimes think now that those years long ago were perhaps the most influential in my ministry.

Oxford since then has become a changed place in which, even physically and geographically, the old-timer can hardly find his way about. How far the vast numerical increase is compatible with its characteristic ethos, only those who work there can judge. Not a few dons, I think, feel misgivings. One cannot help noting that sixth-formers of the highest quality and potential are not always putting down Oxbridge as their first choice: the colleges have to go out and advertise in order to attract the best candidates. Can it be that in trying to modernise itself it has sacrificed what it did supremely well to doing less well what others have told it to do? Whether more necessarily means worse, is a question which only experience can answer; though there is, I should imagine, an optimum size for any institution of higher learning which inherits the university tradition. Certainly a sudden, enforced expansion has gone far to frustrate the visions of its founders in at least one of the post-war universities. I wonder at times whether the Robbins report and the mushroom proliferation of universities before there was any deep consideration of what universities are meant to be, and before there was an adequate supply of junior staff of the required calibre, may not come in future to be re-regarded as a social and educational disaster. What proportion of those who go to university are fitted for university education? For it seems to do some of them a great deal of harm.

It is possible to disseminate knowledge, which can be done by electronic transmission without any human presence at all, but without communicating wisdom or any real understanding of life, leaving the student mentally immature, at the mercy of half-baked slogans and prejudices. But knowledge is no substitute for wisdom, and wisdom is what universities are *for*, a wisdom acquired in some shared community life. Surely a graduate ought to be a man who has achieved some thought-out moral standard, some discrimination of values, some power of discerning between truth and falsehood, some vision of the ends of living — a man with a liberality of mind and some idea of what it is to be truly human.

I am *not* suggesting that higher education should be reserved for a privileged minority. No Christian could possibly stand for that; it is a prime concern of Christianity that it should be spread on the widest possible scale, and I am not unaware of the difficulties. The question is whether this can best be done by crowding everyone into universities. The universities ought to set the standard. And I still believe that the ancient model embodied at Oxbridge, St. Andrews and elsewhere, had something archetypal about it. There is no distinction which I value so much as that, ten years after I left St. Mary's, Oriel made me an honorary fellow.

To my great delight, my old friend F. A. Cockin was persuaded to succeed me at St. Mary's, where he exercised a still remembered ministry. In due course he went on to a canonry at St. Paul's and eventually to the bishopric of Bristol.

VII

Westminster

I INDIAN SUMMER

ONCE AGAIN IT was to be a double job, for the canonry was annexed to a parish. It was put about, when I became a bishop, that I had had no parochial experience. They thought that St. John's was like a city church, with a parish containing little more than Smith Square, with only a tiny, affluent population. In fact, the parish covered a big area, running down Marsham Street to the Tate Gallery and including all those blocks of Council flats, with a huge working-class population. The civil parish, of course, was much bigger still. At that time St. Margaret's and St. John's between them comprised nearly the whole of inner Westminster, and the rectors were prominent figures in civic life. I believe that the parish gained, in the long run, by having one of the Canons for its rector; and have no doubt that the Abbey gained a great deal by association with some of its poorer neighbours. But it meant that during his periods of residence the rector was virtually an absentee. My predecessor in the combined posts had been the fabulous Clifford Woodward ('Wooders') — a man of immense, self-consuming energy and the greatest parish priest of his generation, who is still today a name to conjure with among the older parishioners of St. John's. To succeed him was a challenging task for any man. I was at his consecration as Bishop of Bristol in the Abbey on the morning of Ascension Day, 1933, and installed at Evensong that same afternoon.

All the posts I have held have brought happiness and all have been, each in its own way, rewarding. But none of them have I *enjoyed* quite so much as that to which I had now been commissioned. To find oneself a canon of Westminster, gathered into that great stream of history in which Church and Nation have grown up together, and to feel that in some new sense one belongs to it and has become personally involved in it, is at once exalting and humbling. The Abbey is perhaps the supreme symbol of the continuity of the life of England and of the place of the Church in that life, "alike in prosperity and in adversity". In the dark, testing years that were to come — though as yet few of us had any inkling of them — it inspired faith, courage and endurance.

We are told that the Church is burdened with ancient buildings which no longer serve any useful Christian purpose and may even hinder its witness and its mission. But that seems to me to be talking great nonsense. It is obvious that, with a shifting population, many parish churches may become redundant. If the need they were built to serve has ceased to exist, and no other good purpose can be found for them, let them be pulled down and the proceeds invested in a new church for another population. I have acted on that pretty frequently myself. But this is altogether a different matter. A great national shrine like the Abbey, or St. Paul's or Canterbury or York or the other ancient cathedrals, speak to men of the things that are eternal and bear witness to the Christian presence at the heart of the whole life of a community in a way that, as things now are, no local church can. Were the Abbey now to be given over and secularised, the moral and spiritual consequences in national life could hardly fail to be devastating. It would be like a public confession by the Church that what it stands for, no longer matters.

When a new canon is put into his stall he is admitted into that great inheritance. But if he should cherish any delusions about his own relative importance, or think "what a clever boy am I to have got here", let him stand for five minutes before the high altar, one frail mortal amid all that grandeur, and a sense of due proportion will be restored to him. Where everything speaks of mystery and transcendence he will not long be "exalted over much."

The Abbey, in the splendour and dignity which had been so finely developed by Dean Ryle and owed so much to the Sacrist, Jocelyn Perkins, was an inspiration in which to worship. I do not greatly love cathedral services, which are bound to be rather impersonal and remote, allowing the congregation so small a part; and I do not think I could ever have been a dean, sitting through them twice every day in the year. But here, at its best, was that austere magnificence which is characteristic of the Church of England and which it has so uniquely achieved; and the alternation of Abbey residence with the congregational services in St. John's seemed to be an ideal combination. I rejoiced in the great public occasions, in many of which it fell to me to take part, culminating, in 1937, in the Coronation of George VI and Elizabeth — the more joyful, perhaps, and the more uplifting because of the pain and anxiety preceding it in the tragedy of the Abdication.

It so happened that I was in residence for some of the great obituary occasions — the memorial for Edward Grey, for example, and the funeral of Rudyard Kipling who, on the advice of the Prime Minister (Baldwin, his cousin) was buried in Poets' Corner. For the former, the Dean being on holiday, Dearmer and I seized the opportunity of improving the rather dull and lifeless form which had long been standard for these services, and introduced to the public Spring Rice's hymn, now so well known, 'I vow to thee my country'. Towards the end of my time I was made Custodian and responsible for the complicated business, with all its elaborate precedents and protocols, of seating the multitudes on state occasions. During my last few months I was sub-dean.

The preaching demanded arduous preparation, and I never ceased to find it extremely terrifying. But if a man has something to say and believes it to be of Christian importance, there can be few churches in the world in which it is more worth while to attempt to say it. From there his sound can go out into all lands. At least, I took a great deal of trouble with it.

But having now moved from Newman's pulpit we found

ourselves living in Charles Kingsley's house — which entailed a
certain realignment of loyalties! Our new home, No. 6 Little
Cloister, as it was before the destruction of the next war, was
one of the most beautiful in London — a gracious and perfectly
lovely Queen Anne house (and thus contemporary with St.
John's), looking out one side on to the fountain, on the other,
flooded with sun most of the day, through high sash windows
into the Abbey Garden. The drawing-room, the showpiece of
the house, had a famous Grinling Gibbons ceiling. We have
never had any home to compare with that one. And as people
then still employed domestic service, we could enjoy it instead
of being burdened by it. Here, soon after we had settled in, our
daughter Rosemary was born and was baptised — a privileged
child indeed — before the shrine of Edward the Confessor.
Mervyn Haigh and Cyril Garbett were her godfathers.

The Dean at the time was Foxley Norris ('Old Bill') — a
Yorkshireman who had once been vicar of Halifax. I knew
him quite well, for when he was Dean of York he had been a
staunch ally of Knutsford, and when I went to St. Mary's he
had done something with the Church Commissioners to increase
the income. To me he was always kindness itself; but the
Chapter was not a very happy ship. Indeed, it was plain even
to the newcomer that it was divided by a long-standing tension
between the Dean and Canon Vernon Storr. As a wisecrack
had it about the famous quarrel of Barth and Brunner, what they
disagreed about was what it was about which they disagreed.
Ostensibly it was about Chapter finances. But it was due, I
fancy, to some deep and half-irrational clash of personal
temperament. But why vex their ghosts? All this is now forgotten. The Abbey embraces the ashes of both of them. And,
as Virgil said with so profound a pathos about the battles
between the swarms of bees:

Hi motus animorum atque haec certamina tanta
pulveris exigui iactu compressa quiescent.[1]

[1] Virgil, *Georgics*, IV.86. John Rawlinson quoted those lines when I
showed him the tomb of Mary and Elizabeth — 'regno consortes et urna'.

Storr was himself a most lovable and gifted man, leader of that liberal evangelicalism which has meant so much in the life of the Church of England but seems now to be so sadly lacking in it. It is badly in need of another Storr today, but no one has ever taken his place. Yet his great ability never quite paid off. The second volume of his important work on the theological development of the nineteenth century remained unwritten. This was partly due, no doubt, to poor health. But Storr and I had much in common and his death during the war was a personal loss.

A man of strikingly handsome appearance and in style and bearing unquestionably patrician, Canon Carnegie, Rector of St. Margaret's and chaplain to Mr. Speaker, belonged more to the Edwardian past than to the century of the common man. He seemed now to be resting on his laurels. He had previously been Rector of Birmingham and had there married the widow of Joseph Chamberlain (Neville Chamberlain being therefore her stepson) who brought him wealth and the entrée into the world of political society. That world frequented their house in Dean's Yard, where they maintained a considerable state. There were those who held that he did too little work. But he carried an air of distinction about with him and had at least a very high sense of what was required by his position. Whatever he was, he was not a mediocrity. He took no great part in the business of Chapter. When he did, it could be predicted with certainty that his vote would not be cast for an innovation. Mrs. Carnegie was a queenly figure of indescribable charm and fascination. Though she always remained very much a *grande dame*, she was never in any degree unapproachable. She had a gift for making you feel at once that you were one of her most valued friends.

Canon Lewis Donaldson was an all-out Labour man. He had done a great job as vicar of St. Mark's, Leicester, and had led the march of the unemployed to London. When Ramsay MacDonald appointed Barnes to Birmingham he put Donaldson into the vacant canonry. Here he preached with great conviction and courage a rather old-fashioned social gospel to a not-too-responsive congregation. It was a very good thing for the Abbey, so much involved with the high and mighty, to have this protest kept alive in its councils. For years he held the office of treasurer, and guarded the finances of the Chapter like a dedicated little dragon. It may be inherent in human nature that a treasurer who holds the purse-strings tightly may at times be at loggerheads with his colleagues.

The other canon was Percy Dearmer, an enigmatic and many-sided genius, who had made his name as Vicar of Primrose Hill, and was widely known in the Church as author of *The Parson's Handbook*, as editor of *Songs of Praise*, and for much else. He had been shamefully treated by authority and for years was left without any employment at all except a part-time curacy at Chelsea. A group of clergy, of whom I was one, headed by William Temple, had taken the step of sending a letter to the Prime Minister asking that some preferment might be found for him; and the canonry was the perfectly right response to it. He made a great contribution to the Abbey through improving its ceremonial and its furnishings, and, in particular, it was his initiative which started that work of cleaning the interior which has now been so gloriously completed.

In the course of the next few years there were many changes, but this was the Chapter to which I was admitted. Harold Costley White (afterwards Dean of Gloucester) was headmaster of Westminster school, which is part of the collegiate foundation. The organist, Ernest Bullock, lived next door to us.

The Church of England is not a 'gathered' Church. As the ancient Church of the English people and an integral part of the constitution, it accepts a responsibility for the whole nation. I learnt many things during my time at Westminster, and not the least was a deepened conviction about the place of the Church in national life. Nowhere is that more vividly brought home to one. It is what the Abbey is saying day by day. The parish church serves its own local community; the ministry of the Abbey is to the whole nation and to all sorts and conditions of men within it—a fact which was imaginatively emphasised by the present Dean and Chapter in the arrangements of its nine hundredth anniversary year. If the Church shrinks away from national life and retreats behind its own perimeter, it tends to become self-conscious and devitalised, uncertain of its faith and its mission and preoccupied with its internal politics. Is not that sadly evident at this moment? The slogan 'Let the Church be the Church' may be little more than a rationalised defeatism.

We are told that England has ceased to believe in God, and we hear a great deal about the decline of Church membership. What is striking in our pluralist society is the stubborn persistence of religious belief. Only five per cent of the population wish to record themselves as unbelievers. And another equally striking fact is this, that whatever line the investigator follows, one result seems to be almost constant. Between sixty and seventy per cent identify themselves with the Church of England. Say what you will about 'C of E' or about 'the Church that most people stay away from', it seems to me that this is massive evidence of the hold which the Church still has, or has potentially, if only it would take heart of courage and go out to buy up the opportunity, instead of indulging in spiritual masochism or wallowing in self-depreciation.

But national life is composed of the groups comprising it, and the life of the national Church is composed of its parishes. What the Abbey was teaching me just by being itself, I had to try make come true at St. John's. Despite the mobility of the population and that denigration of the parochial system which is now fashionable among progressives, it remains true and probably always will, that the strength or weakness of the Church in England is the strength or weakness of its local parishes. And that means, in practice, that everything depends on the future quality of its parish priests.

St. John's had to serve a population which seemed to belong to two different worlds. Inner Westminster, in those days, retained something like the atmosphere of a village and was really almost a self-contained community. The great baroque church in Smith Square, with the charming little Georgian streets which opened out of it or led into it, looked like an eighteenth-century period piece. It could almost have come out of a Canaletto. Though Transport House was already in one corner it was then almost wholly residential. Lord Trent lived in the Old Rectory, now rebuilt as Conservative Headquarters. Only about a generation previously the area had been redeemed from slumdom to become an exceedingly fashionable quarter inhabited by the wealthy and distinguished. Because it was within reach of the division bell it was much sought after by prominent politicians, and quite a few members of the Cabinet lived within a stone's throw of the church. One was, therefore, brought constantly into touch with interesting and stimulating people, which was one of the major perquisites of the job. It would be boring to give a list of names, many of them now written into history, and I do not want to appear as a scalp-hunter, but they were distinctly important. In Westminster Gardens at one time there was even Winston Churchill himself. Westminster Hospital was being built on the old churchyard (St. John's Gardens) and, apart from the huge business offices such as ICI and Imperial Tobacco, St. John's included among its parishioners the Church Commissioners and the Mothers' Union, to say nothing of the SPG (or Wippells!), the UMCA and other Church societies. There was plenty of variety in the village! Here was enough to keep a man fully occupied in a highly specialised form of pastoral ministry.

But this was but half, or less than half, of the whole scene. Once across Horseferry Road you were in a different world altogether. A few years before there had been a disastrous flood when the river had come right over the Millbank area and ruined many of the poorer dwellings, with a great deal of suffering and loss. In this disaster Woodward had been the hero, challenging principalities and powers to make good the loss and provide new homes for his people. This led to intensive re-housing and to the existing LCC estate had now been added a Westminster City estate (the high chessboards) in and around Page Street.

In these two estates there was a population numbering, I think, somewhere about 8,000, which was the field for our parochial ministry as then generally understood. Many of them were in low-paid occupations and some were living below the poverty line. There was no national insurance then and the Church had to function as relieving officer, raising all the money it could in Smith Square in order to disburse it in Page Street. Beyond that, of course, there was the familiar programme of visiting, clubs, countless organisations, a large Church school (infant and junior) and all the apparatus of a 'poor' parish. Woodward had left it brilliantly organised and it was a breathless task to keep up his pace. I was helped, from the first, by Christopher Hildyard, a minor canon at the Abbey, where he is still now the venerable Sacrist, and Geoffrey Harding (now Secretary of the Church Council for Health and Healing) who was joined, before long, by Joseph McCulloch, now Rector of St. Mary le Bow. Other curates followed, of whom more later on. But how were these two worlds to be brought together?

At Cranley Gardens Woodward had built his ministry almost entirely round a children's service, and he was an absolute genius with children. He followed the same strategy at St. John's where his children's broadcasts were famous. These I inherited from him and continued, broadcasting from the church one Sunday a month. At these at least there was some social mixing. I can think of at least one heir to a peerage who used to be brought to them by his parents. Otherwise, St. John's was too much a case of the 'two nations'.

But after we had been there about a year and I was just beginning to learn the job, a distinctly exciting letter arrived from Lambeth. Archbishop Lang wanted me to go to Melbourne as representative of the Church of England at the forthcoming centenary of the diocese, and had asked the Dean and Chapter to make it possible. (Colleagues would have to take on my residences.) When I sounded the PCC about it, instead of protesting that they were being sacrificed, they said that the invitation was an honour to them. In order to meet the travelling expenses, the Archbishop of Melbourne nominated me to the Moorhouse lectureship in his cathedral, which carried a stipend of £300; and in those blessed days that amount would buy two first-class returns to Australia! But if I were to go, what about the parish? Lambeth had thought that one out in advance. It happened that Bishop Willis of Uganda – who should be remembered with Llewellyn Gwynne as one of the great apostolic missionaries – was shortly coming back on a four-month furlough and wanted a home during his stay in England. He could therefore take over our house as a going concern and supervise the parish. This seemed a wholly admirable arrangement.

At this point there was a mildly comic interlude. The Australians, it seemed, were affronted at not being offered an English bishop. They wanted somebody far more important than I was, who could be properly dressed up for the part. The Archbishop then persuaded David of Liverpool to come too and take the ceremonial part, while I did most of the talking and gave the lectures; and this would give him a badly needed holiday. So everyone concerned now seemed happy, and having arranged to park Rosemary with her Nanny at her Godmother's house in Oxford, we set out on our first visit to Australia.

We went overland, to join the ship at Naples, so that I could show Lilian something of Rome en route. David was on board and made the voyage with us. The British Empire was still in its might. Everywhere the invincible fleet was in evidence, a British passport was like a magic carpet and it was not yet a liability either to be white or to be an Englishman. Twenty-five years later we made the same voyage, and found that we had to obtain a special permit even to go ashore at Port Said. *Civis*

Britannicus sum meant almost nothing. It can be seldom that an imperial world-power has fallen in so suddenly and so swiftly.

The canal was of course familiar to me already. The exciting moment to me was the passage through the strait out of the Red Sea where the horn of Africa curves round towards Asia and coal-black Somalis come out in their boats to meet you. We spent a day at Colombo with John Campbell, then headmaster of Trinity College, Kandy, with whom we were to stay on the return journey, delighting in the frangipani and the spicy breezes. and the paddy fields 'dressed in living green', and so on towards Western Australia. On the ship with us was General Fabian Ware, chairman of the Imperial War Graves Commission, with whom and his wife we developed a warm friendship. At Fremantle we were met and entertained by an unsuspected colony of Barrys. Long years before my grandfather's elder brother had emigrated to seek his fortunes, and after a perilous voyage in a sailing ship, in the course of which they were blown into Buenos Aires, had finally cast anchor in the Swan River. He went ashore where the city of Perth is now, established himself and founded a family, of which these distant cousins were the descendants. We were to find others in other parts of the continent. Thence we continued by sea round to Melbourne.

We were told to put on robes before arrival, and there was a ceremonial drive – David satisfactorily episcopal – to a civic welcome. I very quickly discovered that in Australia a Lord Bishop really was then a Lord Bishop. David and I had to enter by separate doors and were not allowed to use the same cloakroom — there is one flesh of bishops, another flesh of priests. I derived some amusement from this archaic protocol.

We stayed with the Archbishop, F. W. Head, Guards' padre in France in the first war (and inevitably known as Freddy Tail) and tutor of Emmanuel College, Cambridge. When the archbishopric was last vacant, very shortly after our marriage, my own name had been one of those put forward, but they very wisely elected him instead. If he was aware of this background history, he was far too delicate to make any mention of it. I gave the lectures and made a great many speeches, both at civic and ecclesiastical functions. There was an immense garden party at Bishopcourt and a great centenary service in the cathedral, though of that I can now remember no details. David then went off on a schedule of his own and soon sailed home again by the Cape route.

We were then sent on to New South Wales, where we were guests of Archbishop Mowll in Sydney and were entertained by him and his wife with the utmost kindness and consideration. There was a heavy programme of speaking, and meetings with clergy in that troubled province, and by this time I was becoming tired and jaded. The Archbishop insisted that we took time off, and we had a wonderful long day out in the bush amid all the strange, fascinating flora and the brilliant birds which we now saw, and heard, for the first time. We had been invited to Government House, Canberra, by the Governor-General, Sir Isaac Isaacs, who was a learned student of Scripture and was always pleased to have parsons to argue with. On the night train from Sydney we shared a compartment with a rising young politician whom the world now knows as Sir Robert Menzies. His Excellency laid himself out to entertain us. Canberra was still in its early stages, and few of the public buildings were yet up. But we saw the sights and were introduced to some of the leading personalities, including the Labour Prime Minister, Mr. Lyons, whom, the following year, I showed round the Abbey. As the Federal Parliament was in session we were allowed to sit on the floor of the house and listen to a debate in the Senate. In short, we were given the full VIP treatment. It happens rarely, but when it does it is fun! I gave a lecture to students of some kind — the university was not yet in being — in a hall dedicated to biology. The centre-piece, as it were the numinous object, was a skeleton of the duck-billed platypus; I hoped that the theology I offered them was at least not so obsolete as that. Later I saw one alive in an aquarium, bird, fish and mammal, a strange primaeval organism. And after our return to Victoria we were duly introduced to the Koalas. The final week we spent in Gippsland and received a number of civic welcomes in little up-country towns in the outback, accompanied by 'Waltzing Matilda'. This was our only glimpse of the Australia that one does not see in the great metropolitan coast cities.

We had Christmas at sea on the return voyage. It was oppressively hot and extremely rough. I gave them Holy Communion in the morning; but when the captain called us into his cabin and insisted on our celebrating with him in port and brandy, we nearly passed out. At Colombo John Campbell was waiting for us and drove us up to Kandy to spend a week with him and his sister, Mary, amid that all that wonderful and historic beauty. Ceylon, I think, is one of the few places which is even better than one's expectations. In the temple, I had my first direct contact with the ceremonials of Buddhist worship. This was an immensely educational week.

We broke the journey again at Port Said. Bishop Gwynne had nominated me to preach the annual Gordon memorial sermon; and in those days the government of the Sudan gave the preacher a free return ticket with a quarter-fare ticket for his wife! The journey up the Nile to Khartoum was entrancing, and we had ten days with the beloved Bishop, seeing as much of his work as was practicable and learning from one meeting after another how dominant was the place he held in the trust and affection of the whole community. The record of the Sudan civil service, about as fine a job as ever was done, was largely due to his Christian leadership. While we were at the Clergy House, there arrived a group of men and women from England, coming out as CMS missionaries to open up new fields in the pagan south. The Christianisation of the Nilotic tribesmen and the growth of an indigenous church in the space of a single generation is surely one of the epics of Christian history. Few things have caused me more distress than the overwhelming of so much of his work in the Southern Sudan during its time of troubles. (The cathedral at Juba was built as his memorial.)

From Port Said we came rapidly overland by Naples. So at length we arrived back in Little Cloister and took over our home from Bishop Willis. It had been for us a wonderful experience. This is the kind of travel in which one *learns* things, not a Bingo cruise or a package holiday. It gave us a very much widened vision and we knew much more about the world, and the world-wide Anglican communion, than we had known when we started out. We were lucky indeed to have had this opportunity, and, except that we wanted our baby girl so badly, we had thoroughly enjoyed every minute of it. When I asked Bishop Willis how he had fared, his reply was that "coming as I do from a Christian country", he had been depressed by the poverty of English religious life, as seen in London.

The substance of what I had tried to say in Melbourne, with some other material now long out of date, was published as *The Relevance of the Church.* Not long after St. Andrews university conferred on me an honorary doctorate. I am proud to be a graduate of St. Andrews; and from time to time since I have been invited to preach a university sermon in that lovely and hospitable city.

But now it was time to get back to work. I preached in St. John's the first Sunday evening and told them something of what we had learnt of the place of Christianity in the wide world. Could we help them to realise the vision? The staff had kept the parish going splendidly. They moved shortly and I had then the help of David Worth (now Senior Lecturer at Chelsea Training College), and either then or later, of Patrick Wild, now Rector of Theydon Bois. His father, then Bishop of Newcastle, had previously been Provost of Southwell – a shadow, for me, of unknown things to come.

In the morning, attendances began to increase, and in the course of the next two or three years the church had come to be filled on Sunday mornings with a large congregation from all over London, seeking help, through the sermons and the worship, in finding their way to a relevant Christian faith. Preaching to them made an exacting claim. From Woodward I had inherited among other things the office of chaplain to St. Paul's Girls' school, where I took the annual confirmation classes for a group of highly intelligent young women—which led to taking their weddings a few years later. The boarders, at Bute House, came to St. John's on Sundays, with their remarkable warden, Janet Cunningham, friend and ally of a whole generation of parents. These girls kept the congregation young—and by the same token, the preacher on his toes. Even now we are still in touch with some of them. As Rector, I was also chairman of the governors of the Greycoat school— not yet, as I write, forced into comprehensiveness; and that carried with it responsibility for its daughter, Queen Anne's school, Caversham. I once showed the Queen Mother round Greycoat and many years later she still remembered her visit.

The people who came to St. John's on Sunday mornings were not the inhabitants of Smith Square; and as nearly all the 'residential' element were away in the country at weekends, it was exceedingly difficult to reach them or bring them within the influence of its teaching. To meet this, we started the St. John's lunch club, to give any who wished regular opportunity of meeting the clergy and one another. To this there was an immediate response, and we met in Caxton Hall once a month for a quick, frugal meal and a talk. There would be anything up to a hundred present. They refused to submit to visiting speakers and insisted that I should do all the talking. How much better I could do it now! This was really my main evangelistic effort and I took endless pains with the preparation.

But even so, these were still a minority. What of those who were bidden and did not come? Print might be read where a voice could not carry. But the Church must not present its message in print in a way that at once suggests that it is third-rate. The *Thorney Isle Review* was my first experiment in parochial (or later diocesan) journalism, changing the old style parish magazine into something more attractive and readable, very well produced and (I hope) fairly well written, something more like a Christian 'review'. A Smith-squarian, Mr. A. D. Power, a partner in W. H. Smith's, looked after the typographical details for me and promised to underwrite the cost of production. Quite soon it was paying its own way and rose to a fairly big circulation, inside the parish and beyond it. 'Everyone', of course, does this kind of thing now, but perhaps we did something to introduce the new style.

In its more narrowly parochial aspects the work at St. John's was uphill all the way, and at times disappointing and discouraging. I know well that this must have been partly due to failures in leadership on my side. We had no spectacular 'results' to point to. Like all parsons, we nearly broke our hearts because more people did not come to church. Perhaps we did not fully understand, what has since been so clearly analysed, why it was that the workers were 'alienated', nor the law, now established, of inverse proportion between size of population and response. Moreover, in common with all urban parishes, we were up against the problem of flats and tenements with their social and psychological consequences. But churchgoing provides no true index of success or failure in the Church's ministry. Before we pontificate about the Church's failure we might ask what we should mean by its success. What kind of 'success' had its Founder been? Ministry, after all, means ministry. Did our Lord perform his works of healing in the hope of attracting more recruits for the synagogue? He helped people because they needed help. If we were allowed to take succour and good cheer to many in need, whether physical or spiritual, that, after all, was what we were there for, even though they might not turn up at Evensong. I would never agree to writing that off as 'failure'. And perhaps we may claim not to have failed entirely in turning an area into a Christian neighbourhood, looking to the church as its focal centre. It is a joy to us now to be recognised by older, still-surviving parishioners.

All this time our home in Little Cloister was a perfectly ideal centre for one's more directly personal ministry. It gave pleasure to anyone to be invited there. We did our share of modest entertainment; it gave our guests, we found, keen enjoyment to be taken round the Abbey by moonlight; and we were ourselves invited out more often than at any other time, either before or since. And all this had a more than merely 'social' reference. Moreover, placed in the very heart of Westminster, No. 6 became a kind of lodging house for people coming up from outside London for Convocation or Church Assembly. Haigh and Garbett frequently spent nights with us. George Bell, Williams of Carlisle ('the burglar'), Edward Woods, William Temple himself, would look in, dying for a cup of tea. During my residences, the Abbey preacher and perhaps his wife would be with us for the weekend. Thus there was all the time forming round us an ever-widening circle of friends. The friendships that grow out of his pastoral ministry are the parson's reward; and these are the ones that last best.

All in all, I think we should say in retrospect that these years were the happiest in our lives. Incidentally, this was the only time in which we were not harassed by financial stringency and were given money enough to do the job.

But that Indian summer was only a kind of interim. The ice was coming back over all that world.

2 WESTMINSTER IN WAR

Only the blind could have failed to see it coming. Yet the trouble was that too many Englishmen, and among them too many Christians, had been blind. "The unnecessary war," Churchill called it; and it is possible that with clearer vision and more realistic moral judgement the second world war might have been avoided. Archbishop Ramsey has remarked somewhere that with few exceptions — Gore was one and Principal Forsyth was another — the clergy appear to have thought of the first war not so much as a sign of impending Judgement

as of a temporary, however painful, interruption in the march
of 'progress' and the steady advance of the Kingdom of God on
earth. Even after that war too many Christians were living in a
moral fool's paradise. We shut our eyes to the 'mystery of
iniquity'. We could not or would not bring ourselves to recognise the demonic forces operative in history or the destructiveness of the powers of evil beneath the surface of our civilisation.
Marx was a better prophet than most of us were. Even when
the risk of war became imminent, some of still thought that it
could be averted by enough 'goodwill' or sufficient 'love'. We
thought of peace too much as the absence of war; and if you
refused to fight or to use armed force, that was a sure way of
preserving peace. When Hitler occupied the Rhineland, I
well remember saying to J. C. (Viscount) Davidson, then a
member of Baldwin's government, "If you allow our people to
be involved once again in the Franco-German quarrel, you
cannot justify it to God or man." Seldom have I said anything
more misguided. For, as we can see now with hindsight, had
there been even a token display of force the German generals
would probably have drawn back and the sequel might not have
occurred at all.

Peace means more than the absence of war. It is the fruit
that grows on the tree of justice. What love of neighbour
implies in this context is to build the structures of international
justice empowered with sanctions, to arm right with might. As
St. Paul said about the Roman empire, there must be that
which 'holds down' the man of sin. To confront the powers of
destruction with 'goodwill' is like trying to quench a volcano
by smiling at it. But Christian opinion was far too prone to
think that the way to preserve peace was by disarmament.
And on that a well-organised Christian lobby concentrated far
too much attention. Dick Sheppard organised the Peace Pledge.
By a constant flow of letters to *The Times* (which William
Temple was rather too ready to sign) by passing resolutions and
in other ways, we brought a strong and, as we can now see,
disastrous pressure to bear on public opinion. I think it must now

be honestly admitted that Christians, and liberals in general, must take some share of responsibility for helping to bring about what they were trying, with the best possible motives, to avert. We thought it possible to believe at once both in the League of Nations and in Disarmament. It needed that war to teach us the hard lesson — and some have not learnt the lesson yet — that letting off Christian emotion is not the same thing as having a Christian policy.

Right up to Munich I was myself a pacifist, as indeed most of the chaplains probably were. In the first war, while I was in uniform, I had been tormented all the time by doubts about its moral justification. Now I used to vow that if war did break out I would use the Abbey pulpit to disseminate 'disloyal' and anti-war sentiments; and I must admit with shame that after Munich I shared in the popular hysteria. Only slowly and painfully did I realise the wickedness of Nazism and Fascism and the moral duty of saving the western world from being enslaved to their obscene dominion. Intensely though I shrank from it and dreaded it, yet when the war came I had no moral doubts.

As Hitler intensified his antisemitism, George Bell laboured to rescue some of its victims and was regularly bringing refugees to this country. I persuaded the parish to take a share in this. St. John's received and entertained a body of non-Aryan Christians, men, women and children, from the Reich and Austria. They were established in the Church Hall and the parish put up the money for their provisions. Some of them were exceedingly gifted people, now deprived of employment in their own countries, who had much to contribute to ours, and soon found jobs by which to support themselves. With some of these I remained in touch for years after. Others, I fear, must have been interned in the panic measures immediately after Dunkirk. While they were with us they were welcome guests who enriched the Christian community of the parish. I am glad to recall that we took part in an enterprise which blessed them that gave and them that took.

(*left*) Manorbier Castle

(*right*) The author: still very young.

Archbishop Davidson (*centre*) with Service candidates, Le Touquet, BEF.

Looking at bombed St John's, Smith Square, with my sister.

Southwell clergy holiday at Skegness.

As the plot of the tragedy moved towards its dénouement, the public mood changed from incredulity that such a thing could possibly happen again to profound anxiety and foreboding. The King and Queen went on a state visit to Canada. Suppose war were suddenly to break out, might they not be submarined or even captured? When, to the immense relief of the nation, they returned in safety, they came to a service of thanksgiving in the Abbey: and it fell to me to be the preacher. I rather felt that the sermon had been a failure — I was too much afraid of saying the obvious thing, and could probably do it a good deal better now. But His Majesty graciously asked to have a copy of it to add to his own record of the tour, so now it is somewhere in the royal archives.

During the later months of that summer preparations for war began to be seen in public.

Just before Munich private citizens began to dig trenches in the London parks. Whitehall buildings were being sandbagged. Rudimentary shelters were being organised. Troops began to appear in the streets. All the horrible past was being repeated. A subaltern marched into Parliament Square leading a platoon with an anti-aircraft gun, which they then put into position on Westminster Bridge. A London bobby walked across to protest. "Don't worry, old boy," said the young man, "there's no danger. She won't go off." And that was about the true state of our preparedness. During the year bought off at Munich, preparations were intensively pushed on, not only in the armament factories but also in plans for civilian defence. It was believed that "the bomber will always get through" and that on the very first night our cities would be overwhelmed in flame and ruin. We lined up to take courses in first aid. (At the one I attended, the first lecture was devoted to the treatment of snake bite — hardly, one supposed, the most likely form of casualty.) Air-raid warden services were organised; and when the crisis came, little men from back streets were to be revealed in heroic stature as leaders and shepherds of their fellows. (Wilkins House commemorates the work of a warden in the

Marsham Street area, who was parish secretary of St. John's.)

I persuaded the Chapter, with some difficulty, that we must provide some shelter for our own college. There were plans for building a canons' garage, but this was hardly the moment for that. They agreed, however, to build a 'garage' in three-foot thick reinforced concrete against the wall of the Abbey garden. There, when the bombing began, the entire Abbey population, Dean, canons and their families, vergers, and everyone, slept night by night in comparative security, while the duty men stood by the telephone. Many owed their lives to that garage. Before the war started Foxley Norris had died and was succeeded by Paul de Labilliere, who sustained and united the whole college through all the tribulations that were to come.

During the first few months, the phoney war, the ministry both of the Abbey and of St. John's could be carried on almost 'as usual'. On the declaration of war the Chapter decided to close down the choir school. London would be no place for small boys. I thought it a little panicky at the time, but in the event it was providential, for in the following winter a direct hit was registered on the choir school buildings. Westminster school was also evacuated. In the Abbey services all through the war there were no boys' voices to be heard. The Prime Minister made a dramatic attempt to strengthen the Abbey for its wartime witness by fetching Hensley Henson out of retirement and persuading him to accept a vacant canonry. It was hoped that his preaching would help to rally the nation. On the very first day of his first residence, when he went to the lectern to read the lesson he found that he could not see the Bible clearly enough; and with characteristic courage and resolution he resigned the same afternoon.

Almost till the war began I had at St. John's two outstanding colleagues, Roger Wilson, now Bishop of Chichester, henceforward one of my closest friends, and Alan Leeke — a young Greek God to behold — who later went down with the aircraft carrier *Hermes*. We maintained Sunday services in the church, did all we could to take hope and courage to those who were fearful or bereaved, and, despite the blackout and other restrictions, still kept up some kind of parochial life.

But, as older readers will remember, there were mounting anxieties and dangers in the spring and summer of 1940. One Sunday evening Brendan Bracken stopped me in Lord North Street on my way to church and told me about the impending surrender of France and its probable consequences for this island. With these good tidings in my ears I went into St. John's to take Evensong. That night we listened to Churchill's famous broadcast. Dunkirk followed. England stood alone, seemingly exposed and defenceless. Invasion seemed now to be almost certain. Children were hastily sent out of London, and cables poured in from the USA offering homes for children for the duration. Anyone who was not required by his war work to stay was urged to leave and those who had country retreats went off to them. (It is a libel to say that the 'upper classes' ran away and bought themselves safety.) Men who were known to be on Hitler's blacklist carried cyanide tablets in their pockets. The Home Guard was recruited—and armed with pikes! The Coronation chair and other treasures were sent away to a secret destination; if Hitler came and demanded to be crowned, he should not sit in the chair of the English sovereigns. The King and Queen rightly refused to leave. And the other people who refused to leave were the wives, who stayed by their husbands.

There was a piece in *Punch* which is worth recalling It ran:

> London Bridge is falling down,
>   My fair lady,
> But you put on your gayest gown,
> Your brightest smile, and *stayed in town*,
> When London Bridge was falling down,
>   My fair lady.

Some years after, when it was all over, I dedicated a new church to St. Martha, in honour of British housewives during the war.

For whatever reason, attack from the air is far more alarming than shellfire on the ground, and air attack on crowded civilian centres is, as it is meant to be, utterly terrifying. I was even more frightened as a civilian parson than I had been before as a chaplain in battle. Yet, I am thankful that during this grim time my work lay in Westminster, in the thick of it. One learnt with a new reverence to what splendour human nature is capable of rising.

During the summer of 1940 there had been some sporadic daylight bombing. But it was not till the autumn of this year that the full weight of the air attack developed.

In September Lilian and I stood breathless in the Cloisters watching the Battle of Britain in the golden skies above our heads. Londoners were gazing up from the streets, cheering, even offering to make bets, as though it were some kind of infernal cup-tie. Evening papers announced the latest scores, treating this decision between life and death as though it were a sporting event. None of us knew then that before the end the last air squadron had been committed. By so narrow a knife-edge were we delivered, at a cost of young lives which one cannot bear to contemplate.

This is not a history of the war. Other cities suffered as much and maybe worse. I am merely recording what I myself experienced.

After the Battle of Britain, the Luftwaffe concentrated on intensive night-bombing. For six months, every night without intermission, except for about two nights of dense fog and, I think, some kind of 'truce' on Christmas Eve, fire and ruin rained down out of the sky. The first night was absolutely appalling. There were no air defences that counted, and although a few shelters had been built these were still too few and rudimentary to provide for more than a small minority. The dense population in the poorer districts, and among them my people of St. John's, had to sit it out, watching their homes destroyed, suffering terror, mutilation and death, without any adequate refuge or protection. (One of our friends was drowned

in a basement.) Early next morning I rang up No. 10 and asked
for an interview with Brendan Bracken. I told him that this
simply would not do. The Government were responsible for
these people. And I added that if this were allowed to go on
there would be anti-war demonstrations which the Government
might not be able to contain. Bracken sent me on to the Home
Office, where I made the same speech with some embellish-
ments, and the Under-secretary wrote it all down. The following night a number of naval guns were mounted on lorries and
sent out into the streets. They were not of the slightest use
against the bombers, but they made an enormous and most
encouraging noise and at least helped people to believe that the
powers-that-be had not abandoned them.

In one part of London or another these raids went on night
after night, increasing in severity and destructiveness. No tribute
can possibly be too high to the Civil Defence personnel, the
wardens, the ambulance men and all the rest, who succoured
their fellows at such great risk to themselves.

My duty, of course, was to be with my parishioners, and
whenever there was an incident in the parish one must be on
the spot and do whatever was possible. Or perhaps one would
spend the night at the hospital, to comfort the casualties as they
were brought in. After a bomb had exploded the sights of
carnage and mutilation were indescribable. In the morning
the streets were strewn with rubble and the wreckage of
homes that had been destroyed, the very abomination of
desolation. For some weeks I did a set of broadcasts, speaking
out of the great tribulation on behalf of the faith that can overcome the world; these were afterwards published as *I Heard a
Voice*. I permitted myself a perhaps unworthy gibe about
"prophets of doom who sit in safe places preparing sermons
about the wrath of God".

During these months there was almost continuous bombing,
in the daylight hours as well as after nightfall. To be out and
about at all was always dangerous and one had to learn to live
with a situation in which, when either of us left the house, he

or she might never come back alive again. ("In the *midst* of
life we are in death".) Londoners told one another bomb stories
as one of the staple subjects of conversation. If they could joke
about it, they could stick it. Workers, bombed in their factories
or offices, might be attacked as they queued at their bus stops
for the dangerous drive through the blackout to their homes,
there perhaps to spend the night in a cellar, if not to be killed
in their beds. Still they carried on and the work never ceased.

I am well aware that there was another side to the 'heroisms'
of civil life in wartime, and this has been often enough exposed in fiction. But human nature seems, broadly speaking, to
show up better under strain and stress than it does when it
is affluent and relaxed. (We have not reduced crime by the
abolition of poverty.)

During all this time the services in the Abbey were maintained
without intermission. It was not without risk, for the Abbey
has no crypt, and there was no shelter for the congregation. If
a bomb had fallen, anything might have happened. I remember
Vernon Storr's funeral service. The siren sounded just as we
were beginning and soon a bomb could be heard just over the
church. As I went to the lectern for the lesson, the ghastly
noise came nearer and nearer, the whole building was quaking,
and it seemed quite certain that the bomb would be crashing
straight through the roof. It needed some self-control to go on
reading, without any audible tremor in the voice, "in a moment,
in the twinkling of an eye" – though one understood what New
Testament writers meant when they spoke about living at "the
last hour". (Their 'eschatology' was literal, not a theological
façon de parler.) But in the end it fell in Parliament Square and
did not explode. There was no disaster.

St. John's was put of action on the first night. Hence-
forth, by the kindness of the SPG, we used their chapel for our
Sunday services. (There was a cellar below it, which gave con-
fidence.) There was always a score or two of worshippers.
Among them were often the CIGS (Sir John Dill) and Air
Marshal Roderic Hill, then living in a Westminster flat,

who, with Helen, his wife, were to become dear friends of ours. No evening service was practicable, partly on account of the blackout, partly also because by that time everybody concerned would be underground. And one's ministry was taking on a new pattern. Some Westminster churches found a new vocation in turning their crypts into houses of refuge. (My friend Austin Thompson was killed, having come up for a moment for a breather, on the steps of St. Peter's, Eaton Square.) Enormous shelters were gradually organised, and at dusk the long procession started, people carrying blankets and bundles and perhaps small children in their arms, into the tube stations or these shelters. In them a strange kind of social life developed and something like a shelter sub-culture. There were many of these in our area, and when possible I would spend some time in one or other of them night by night. In some, bedtime prayers were found to be welcome. In all, one could talk with the people and try to cheer them, and at least show, just by being there, that the Church cared for them because God cared for them. Going round the shelters was now one's nightly task — it often needed all my courage to go — and in close co-operation with William Sangster, at that time Minister of the Central Hall, we developed this new form of pastoral ministry. I think we got nearer to the people that way than ever we had by parochial 'visiting'.

The Abbey was still miraculously undamaged. St. Paul's was the symbol of the soul of London and the Cross still stood above the ruins. The Abbey was in some real sense the symbol of the soul of national life. To preserve it if possible was thus a national as well as an immediate Christian duty. Under Mr. Bishop, clerk of the works, and the registrar, Mr. Hebron, there was a devoted team of fire-watchers who patrolled the church all through every night — and when bombs were falling near by this was an exceedingly hazardous occupation — putting out incendiaries on the roof, preventing a spark from becoming a conflagration. But in the last and worst of the raids on London the Abbey was within an inch of destruction.

On the night of 10th May, 1941, the whole of Westminster seemed to be on fire. The technique was first of all to bomb the water mains. So, when the shower of incediaries came there was no effective means of putting them out. All the houses in Little Cloister caught fire, but at first we were too much concerned with the Abbey to have time to defend our own homes. When at last I got a hose on to No. 6 only a thin little trickle of water came out. Nothing could be done, and the house was burnt to the ground and every single thing we possessed destroyed. Other houses were also on fire; we tried to help to move out some of the valuables but the heat and smoke were becoming too much. The school hall ('School') and other buildings were burnt out and the whole scene was like an inferno. But worst of all, the Abbey was in great danger. The central tower was burning, and if that spread nothing could save the whole church from destruction. The men worked on it fearlessly and incessantly but could not manage to get it under control. The fire brigades were all occupied already and Bishop could get no help from that quarter. But we *had* to get some help before it was too late. So about three o'clock in the morning I got a telephone call through to Downing Street and told them that only the Prime Minister's authority could now save the Abbey from being gutted. The duty officer there sent a brigade along and by morning the fire had been safely brought under control.

By this time the actual bombing had stopped, so Lilian and I went down into the parish. We were homeless and destitute, possessing nothing, not so much as a clean handkerchief or a comb. But we were so thankful at being still together, that the rest did not seem to matter very much. In Smith Square, St. John's was on fire, flames spiralling up through all its four corners. The Old Rectory and much else had been destroyed. Then we went down along Marsham Street to see how many people were still alive. We called, among others, on the Hills, whom we found sleeping on their floor. I got a wash and brush up in their bathroom. I needed it. For this was a Sunday morning and at eight there would be Holy Communion in our chapel. A few half-stunned people had managed to get there. I had only the filthy clothes that I stood up in, cassock and surplice had gone the way of all flesh: and, as I no longer possessed a prayer book, a copy was borrowed from one of the communicants. Roderic and Helen then produced breakfast for us.

The one thing we had now was an ancient car, which had somehow survived the previous night. It looked as thought that car, like a Scythian waggon, would have to be our home for some time to come — assuming, of course, that we could get any petrol for it. The best thing seemed to be to drive to Oxford, where Rosemary had been parked with Lilian's mother. There we could at least get some sleep. But then I remembered that I was engaged to preach that evening at Queen Anne's, Caversham. Why not? It was on the way to Oxford. Again, I had only the same greasy, wet clothes over which I draped the headmistress's gown. I cannot imagine what I managed to say to them, but never have I been listened to so intently.

At Oxford, which was disgustingly safe and prosperous, I went to a shop to buy myself a razor. "A *razor*?" said the disdainful young lady. "Haven't you heard that there is a war on?" I did not explain that I was faintly aware of this, but I felt a strong urge to pick her up and spank her. (The *Spectator* got hold of this incident and worked it up into a wonderful story, but it did rest substantially on fact.) For quite a long time there were two kinds of place and two kinds of people in this country — those who had been bombed and those who hadn't.

A great many other people have been through it and I do not want to make a song and dance about it, but the loss of all your material possessions does create certain immediate problems. Sooner or later you must have a clean shirt and something presentable to go around in. But clothes were strictly rationed, as well as food, and could only be bought against very niggardly coupons. Accordingly, on our return to London, we had to make humble application to a spotty young man enjoying a brief authority for coupons enough for an elementary outfit. I found that interview most enlightening: "Address?" "I have no address at this moment." That was enough; we were homeless persons and could therefore be bullied and put in our proper places. In the end, I got pretty well what was needed. But I learnt then how the poor and most defenceless can be hectored by petty officials, and how understandably they are reluctant to claim reliefs to which they may be entitled.

After 10th May the night-bombing of London ceased and, until the V2s arrived, daylight attacks became far less frequent. Some sort of normality therefore began to come back. We even had one more St. John's lunch, when such few people as could still be collected met for a stand-up meal in Jerusalem chamber, and a caterer managed to provide something that was not too revolting to eat. For ourselves, we were fortunate in securing for a few weeks the sub-lease of a flat in the parish, in Tufton Court where we now live. But that came to an end in July. I was then in an extremely exposed position. With nowhere to live, how could we do the job? Did this mean that I must leave Westminster and accept the first offer that came along which would provide a home for my family? (I did have the courage to refuse one, which would have been quite an honourable way out.) But, by now, we were pretty well exhausted. Come August, therefore, we collected Rosemary and went up to Borrowdale to renew ourselves. While we were there a letter arrived from Churchill offering me the diocese of Southwell. I had received some hints before it came and had had the opportunity to think about it, and now I felt that it was right to accept.

When it was announced, I had a letter from one of the leading parishioners of St. John's at the end of which he asked me a pregnant question. "While you have been here with us," he said, "you have tried to stand for something rather distinctive. Will you still be able to do that as a Bishop?"

VIII

Southwell

I WINTER

I WAS CONSECRATED Bishop by William Temple in York
Minster on St. Luke's day (18th October), 1941. The evening
before, along with Bishop Noel Hudson, who had been
appointed to Newcastle, we submitted, uncomprehending but
fascinated, to the legal ceremony of 'confirmation'. There were
no other new bishops to be consecrated and I felt extremely
small and naked as the procession moved through the vast nave.
But I still remember the thrill and exultation of hearing boys'
voices in the choir again; it suggested passing from death into a
new life. Of course the difficulties of wartime travel kept
away many whom one would have wished to have there. But
some of my closest friends stood beside me. Harry Baines
— himself before long to be Bishop of Singapore — was the
preacher. Cyril Garbett and Herbert Williams (Carlisle)
presented me. (The day before, when Garbett arrived at
Bishopthorpe, he remarked, all unmindful of his doom,
"Thank Heaven I don't have to live in this place.")

At a consecration the Anglican liturgy is seen at its best and
most magnificent; and here one is at the heart of the Church's
life. Surrounded by the witness of all the ages a man is admitted
into the great inheritance and empowered, with all his human
frailties, by being made partaker of what is *given*, coming down
from the Lord of the Church himself. The life of the Church
must always be a tradition, communicating what it has
received. And, despite much that is now being said to the
contrary, it seems to me that its institutional structures must

always retain some hierarchical element, whether that be personal or collegiate, reflecting the givenness of the Christian life. It is not the Ministry that makes the Church, it is the Church that validates the Ministry. The authority committed to the Ministry is the God-given authority of the Church, which is not the clergy but the whole body of Christ. But it is God-given, it comes down from above, and is not, as it were, thrown up from below. The Christian Church is a unique society, and its life in the world can never be rightly organised on the lines of a parliamentary democracy or, for that matter, of a business plant. Bishops are not meant to be organisation men.

Thus at one of the darkest moments of the war, when victory, or even survival, seemed to be mortally in peril and only faith could believe in any future, I entered this new period of my ministry, far longer than any of the others, as leader and pastor of a wartime diocese. This was the greatest day of my life.

During the six or eight weeks before St. Luke's day we had to wrestle with many domestic problems. How could we take over our new home, which contained, reputedly, twenty-six bedrooms, when we did not possess a single stick of furniture? Somehow, the question began to answer itself. A group a laity in the Southwell diocese, before ever they had set eyes on me, sent us a cheque for £600 (at least £3,000 in present values) — a wonderful gesture of understanding welcome. With this we bought what could still be obtained. Kind people in Westminster and in Nottinghamshire offered us all sorts of pieces, some of which we are still using now. A lady who wanted to get it out of London offered us the use, for the duration, of the entire contents of her house. One way and another there was enough to furnish such rooms as we needed for the time being. By a brilliant exercise in logistics, Lilian assembled all this collection, bought, given or lent, from many different places at Bishop's Manor in time for the enthronement. We rejoiced in having a home of our own again in which Rosemary could now be with us.

It was a dignified and gracious house which had been constructed by Bishop Hoskyns in, and out of, the fourteenth-century manor, in a quadrangle formed by the ruins. But, like all the pre-war episcopal 'palaces', it was built to be run by a large staff of servants and my predecessor was full of lamentations because the war had left him with only six; it presupposed unlimited fuel; and it was far too expensive for any Bishop who did not possess 'ample private means'. No layman with £3,000 a year (even pre-war) would have dreamt of attempting to live in it. And as time went on it became a crippling burden. This was of course before the Church Commissioners had come on the scene to look after Bishops' houses. The more recently appointed Bishops have never been introduced to the facts of life. They have had so much laid on free for them, even the cost of moving into the house. We had to find everything ourselves, to furnish the house, decorate and maintain it, and cover all our official expenses — secretary, postages, travelling — as well as keeping up an enormous garden out of an income that simply could not bear it. We could never spend on the job what it needed; my devoted secretaries got sweated wages; and I had to go around in an ancient car which was constantly breaking down by the roadside. After a while, a generous, wealthy layman in the diocese gave me the present of a new car, which he then replaced periodically, secretly and strictly 'anonymously' — I knew who he was and he knew that I knew — and paid a substantial sum into my account year by year on 1st of January. That (bless him) enabled me to carry on. But for that I might well have been forced to resign after only a short time through sheer inability to stand the financial pace. So much for the opulence of pre-war Bishops!

All that is now lifted off the Bishop's shoulders, as it was, towards the end of our time, off mine, when the Church Commissioners took the house over. All his expenses are lavishly provided for — I sometimes wonder, indeed, if not too lavishly. This, however, is rather to anticipate; and I do not want to give the impression that we started off with a grievance or regarded our new abode as a burden. We were thankful to have been given a beautiful home. We were happy there and enjoyed living in it.

On All Saints' Day, 1st November, I was enthroned in my cathedral by the Provost, W. J. Conybeare — a remarkable man of the previous generation, who had been chaplain to Archbishop Frederick Temple. It was a dank and foggy November day. Wartime restrictions and shortages and the preoccupations of the public mood deprived the traditional enthronement service of much of the customary pomp and splendour. But the petroleum officer did his best, and there was a very large congregation. There were even people seated in the triforium. Marcus Tod was there on behalf of Oriel. The Dean, de Labilliere, and others came as representatives of the Abbey, and I was 'pokered' by Drake, the Dean's verger. After he has been placed in his throne and the clergy have passed by and made their bows, the Bishop speaks to his diocese for the first time. Seldom can a man feel so much on trial. It is, in a way, a kind of policy speech. But my opening words were "Christ is risen"; and I tried to give them some hope and encouragement amid all the anxieties of that dreadful time.

It was only a short while after this that the *Prince of Wales* and the *Repulse* were sunk, and Britain had lost command of the sea.

Southwell was not one of the best-known dioceses. Indeed, I have spent quite a lot of time since then explaining to people what I was Bishop of! It was formed only in 1884, partly out of Lincoln, partly out of Lichfield, to compose a diocese for the East Midlands, and included Nottinghamshire and Derbyshire. (Subsequently this had been divided again; and even today there are some in both dioceses who question the wisdom of the separation.) I was only the fifth bishop in the succession. The first had been George Ridding, headmaster of Winchester, who had brought in his Wykehamists to staff the diocese, of whom some were still serving in my own time. He was succeeded by Sir Edwin Hoskyns, then (for a short time) by Bernard

Heywood and my much-loved predecessor, Henry Mosley. So I was very much bishop of a new diocese; and whereas in an ancient diocese the bishop is an institution before he arrives — he may be the ninetieth in succession — in the new he has to earn his position. As I was to find, that may not be too easy. It is not something that he can take for granted.

When it was founded, history seemed to dictate that the seat of the bishopric should be at Southwell. The ancient minster, the 'village cathedral', one of the noblest churches in England, now more widely known than it was then, goes back very nearly to Paulinus. It has always been a secular foundation. Tourists ask, Where did the old monks sleep? But, in fact, there have never been any monks. It was one of the pre-conquest 'minsters' which served the parishes in the surrounding country-side through a collegiate body of priests or 'prebendaries'. Eight hundred years later, the prebendaries of Southwell had become a corporation of wealthy sinecurists. It was suppressed by Sir Robert Peel's commissioners, by whom all the endowments were diverted to found the new diocese of Manchester. It had long associations with York, and certainly before the Norman Conquest the archbishops held the manor of Southwell (see p. 179). Nottinghamshire, then very sparsely populated and mainly forest, was part of the York diocese, administered through the archdeaconry of Nottingham, which is the oldest archdeaconry in England. In the vast mediaeval diocese, the archbishops required a number of local outposts — Beverley, Ripon and Southwell were among them — in which they could establish their *cathedra* as they went around on their visitations, moving from one of their manors to another. So Southwell had always contained an episcopal stool, and it seemed fitting in 1884 to make it the bishop's church for the new diocese. Thus the ancient minster became a 'new' cathedral[1] and the rector of the parish became provost.

[1] 'New' cathedrals are those belonging to modern dioceses, like Guildford, Portsmouth, Bradford, or Southwell itself. The term should not be confused with 'cathedrals of the new foundation', which are those founded or refounded by Henry VIII after the Dissolution.

The diocese coincides with the county boundaries and therefore, though predominantly industrial, it is in no way mono-
chrome or uniform. Indeed, not the least of its attractions is the
rich variety of its human interests. The conurbation of Nottingham itself, with its mixture of textile and heavy chemical
industries, dates from the Industrial Revolution. Beyond it are
the Nottinghamshire coal-fields, of which the town of Mansfield
is capital. There are pleasant rural suburbs south of the city,
reaching out to Leicestershire and the Vale of Belvoir. There
are 'the Dukeries' (mainly without dukes) in what remains of
the ancient Sherwood forest. And north and east, towards
Yorkshire and Lincolnshire, there is a hinterland of agricultural
country — the territory of 'north Notts' farmers' with a number
of quite remote village parishes.

No doubt that may be fairly called a description of any
typical cross-section of England. Yet it was quite a new world
for us. When you cross the Trent you have crossed a cultural
tropic. This was definitely North not South. These seemed to be
people of a different kind — of course they had strongly distinctive tribal origins — and this was a different kind of society
from what we had known at Oxford or Westminster. Living in
Westminster almost unfits a man for living and working in
what it calls 'the provinces'. Some things he has learned there
will have to be unlearnt. It will need a certain mental readjust-
ment before he can fully identify himself with the clergy and
people of the industrial Midlands.

So in every way we were now making a new start.

I was fifty-one now, with experience behind me, and at what
is commonly called the prime of life. But there was an immense
amount to be learnt; and many years would be needed to learn
it. I now had to face a new form of ministry. How did one set
about being a bishop? Long after, when I was quite senior, I
was asked in New Zealand to give a talk, or write a book, on
'how to episcopate'. My reply was that for fifteen years I had
been endeavouring to find out, and was endeavouring to find
out still. Any man who felt he could give a confident answer

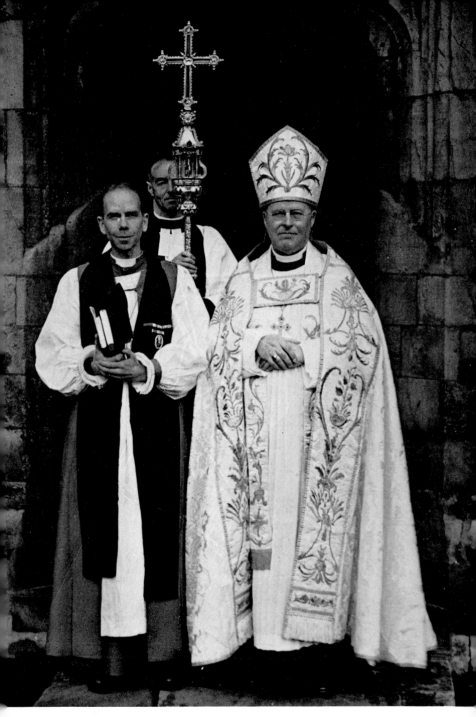

Outside York Minster, 18th October 1941.

At the Church Building, Royal Show, Nottingham, 1955.

would surely be in a dangerous condition. But a new Bishop is virginally innocent. One of the odd things in the Church of England is that, while it takes elaborate care about making a man a deacon or a priest, it does nothing whatever for a bishop. Nobody gives him any advice or coaching or offers him any spiritual counsel. Even William Temple seemed surprised when I asked him at Bishopthorpe the night before the consecration whether he could spare me a few minutes because I wanted his help with certain questions — and they were not merely procedural questions either. (I should add that of course he did give me what I needed.)

The new Bishop is just thrown in at the deep end to sink or swim and learn from his mistakes. And the very next morning after his enthronement he must start to function; he doesn't know what to do, yet he must not give the impression of not being master of the situation. He will have to deal with arrears of correspondence and find himself called upon to give advice "on matters which he does not understand". Some problems — as well as a number of fixed engagements — he will have inherited from his predecessor, and he will have to give decisions about affairs with which he has had no personal acquaintance. All this means that for the first few weeks he is almost entirely dependent on his staff, and must act more or less on their briefing and advice. I offer my tribute of gratitude to those who steered me through my episcopal novitiate.

I mention first Bishop Neville Talbot — a great man of God and a great human being, who was somehow built on lines too outsize to fit into the system of the Church of England, which never discovered how to make proper use of him. His father was Edward Talbot, Bishop of Winchester, the Grand Old Man of the Davidsonian era — one of that senate of patrician Bishops who, with their aristocratic connexions, never doubted that they were called by God to rule others for their good. Neville had fought as a private in the Boer war. He had for some years been chaplain at Balliol, and had then been elected Bishop of Pretoria. When he came back the Church had nothing to offer him, and Henry Mosley seized the chance of securing him as Assistant Bishop and Vicar of St. Mary's, Nottingham. He had been in charge during the interregnum and now handed the diocese back to me. But it was a delicate personal relationship. He had been my ACG in the first war; he was far senior to me and far more experienced; and he may have felt, as I certainly did feel, that our positions ought to have been reversed. He was much too big a man to show any sign of that. He gave me generous welcome and support, and coached me through many difficult situations. He was rather eating his heart out at St. Mary's and needed a much wider field of manœuvre. But he died before the war had ended. There is a tablet to him in St. Mary's.

The Archdeacon of Newark, Percy Hales, was one of Bishop Ridding's young men and had spent his whole ministry in the diocese. Winchester and Cambridge (not Oxford) written all over him, he was one of that splendid type of priests which is now becoming far too rare in the Ministry — one of those "gentlemen in holy orders" whom the new-style ordinands tend to undervalue. He had been a DACG in the first war — about which, even now, he was still talking! Brought up to a more gracious style of manners, he would have thought it almost morally wrong to sit down to his dinner without having 'dressed', even though, as was probable in wartime, it would be dinner of spam or whale-steak. He was a sportsman, clubbable and forthcoming, and had an immense influence with the laymen. But he was withal a dedicated priest and deeply serious about his ministry. He stood by me, guided me, coached me, drove me around — a true friend and an honest critic. I cannot easily say how much I owed to him.

The Archdeacon of Nottingham, Victor Turner, was a Nottinghamshire man born and bred, and knew the whole diocese inside out. He had been my predecessor's right-hand man, and he put his knowledge completely at my disposal. Without it I should hardly have been able to deal with some unexpected situations. One of the first things he made me do was to extricate two clergymen from a libel action. He left us quite soon to become Bishop of Penrith.

Noel Turner, Bishop Mosley's chaplain, continued to serve me in that capacity. He helped a great deal by showing me the way about and introducing me to the right people. He was Rector of Epperstone when he joined me and Rector of Epperstone he is still today.

All Saints' Day that year was on a Saturday. It so happened therefore that my first public appearance was to preach next morning at the annual service of what was then University College, Nottingham. On any long-term view of Christian strategy this was the most important place in the diocese. And Principal Wortley had already told me how much the college would welcome the new Bishop if he could show that the Church had something to offer it and that he was able to understand its problems. Much preparation had gone into that sermon! This led to fairly frequent invitations and I came to know Wortley very well, and through him, some of the leading figures in the work of planning the new university. I was allowed to be unofficially in on that, and was able, in particular, to ensure that the Department of Christian Theology was incorporated in the original charter, not added on later as an afterthought; and shall always be glad to have taken some part in the birth of the Nottingham Faculty of Theology, which has since become so distinguished. Wortley did not live to see his dream come true. He and his wife died in the same week shortly before the charter was issued, and I took a joint funeral in St. Mary's. But I was on friendly terms with Bertrand Hallward, first vice-chancellor of the University, with whom I co-operated in many projects, not least the establishment of the chaplaincy. Though I was careful never to claim any 'rights', I was frequently asked to the university and throughout my time was closely associated with it. We were even asked to the undergraduates' ball and always went, even in the snowstorms by which it seemed to be fatefully accompanied. Eucharists on occasional Sunday mornings and confirmations in the crypt chapel are among my happiest recollections. I was proud and delighted when the university conferred on me its honorary doctorate of divinity, the only one, I think, that it has ever given, and it was an added pleasure to receive it from my former parishioner, Lord Trent, almost by hereditary right first chancellor of the new university. I doubt whether in any other diocese the Church then enjoyed more admirable relations with its local university than we enjoyed, during my episcopate. So that first Sunday morning was not unfruitful.

Now I had to start getting about the diocese. But in wartime, of course, everything was against you. I was given a certain allowance of petrol but it had to be husbanded like liquid gold, and I did quite long distances on a pushbike and even on foot to save what little there was. (During the war, oil was struck in Nottinghamshire, a few hundred feet below the coal measures, and was being pumped and despatched in substantial quantities, though this was veiled in security precautions. We were not supposed to know anything about it.) But petrol was only a part of the difficulty. This was as yet completely unknown territory, and the signposts had all been removed; finding the way about was extremely baffling. At night, the blackout made it quite impossible, and unless someone was willing to transport me I could not risk being out after dark. But with help from Noel Turner and many others I did manage to cover most of the area, to find out at least where the parishes were, and to meet some of the more prominent laymen and at least the incumbents of the key parishes, particularly of course the rural deans, on whom I was to rely more and more.

Many units of the Forces were stationed in the diocese — in this most landlocked county of England there was even at least one naval establishment — and one first, obvious duty was to to look after them. So I spent a good deal of time in those early days in army camps and RAF stations, and in taking confirmations for the chaplains. At the big central confirmations which were customary in the minster on Ascension Day there were always a number of men and women in uniform, which made the service peculiarly impressive — though I am convinced that in general principle it is a mistake to mix adults up with children. Confirmation, for adults, means something rather different; and the whole effect is spoiled if the service, and not least the Bishop's address, are designed primarily for adolescents. Special centres ought to be provided for them.

Many of the clergy were away as chaplains. The best known of them, Hughes, Monty's chaplain in Africa and afterwards Chaplain General to the Forces, was absent from Mansfield during the whole of the war. So the parishes were grievously undermanned. Many laymen too were away in the forces, and those who remained were preoccupied with war work. The tide of the war had not yet begun to turn, and a cloud of anxiety lay on the spirits of all of us. But there was no such total disruption of church life as one had known in London. This was a comparatively 'safe' area. There had been one severe raid on Nottingham in which two churches had been destroyed, but elsewhere they had suffered little damage. The Church was in being, though with a diminished vitality. The task was to try to keep Christians in good heart, to endeavour to make the Church count as a power-house of courage and hope to a hard-pressed people, and prepare for the time when life should open up again.

One of my earliest problems was financial. The chemical industry (Boots) and the clothing factories, to say nothing of coal-mines, were working at high pressure, and many people had money to burn in their pockets. But little of that came the way of the clergy. There were still too many shamefully low-paid benefices. Some of the clergy were desperately poor, and I quickly discovered that inside the vicarages there were families living below the poverty line and who could hardly afford enough to eat. They were, as always, brave and uncomplaining; but they had enough to struggle against without that. There were no Church Commissioners' grants then, no official ways of improving stipends. No long-term solution was yet feasible.

But something urgent had to be done at once. An emergency fund had to be made available. The laymen gave me a large sum of money to be used as income rather than capital, to tide over the immediate crisis. Out of this annually, while the war lasted, we distributed what were in effect doles, though disguised as Christmas presents from the laity, to those clerical homes where they were most needed.

This was 'relief', or charity in the wrong sense, and in some ways a humiliating business; but just then and there nothing else could be done. Radical solutions had to wait. Of course we were merely alleviating symptoms – though when one is ill the symptoms are what hurt. But at least we gave some small timely help to men too proud and long-suffering to ask for it, and saved some wives from defeat and breakdown. And perhaps it cheered some of them to be shown in this small way that the diocese cared about them. I had not forgotten my own parsonage childhood.

But this was no more than one man's initiative, and an *ad hoc* effort that could not be repeated; it was no way to tackle the problem that was still left. The diocese now began to make experiments in the permanent augmentation of stipends, and did as much as it could with what we had. I am glad that we were among the first in the field, before central authority took action. A few years later Archbishop Fisher weighed in with his 'challenge' to the Church at large, the Commissioners started to do financial miracles, and the whole question was put on an official, public and self-respecting basis.

In response, the diocese worked hard and generously, and now it was the time to transfer the answer from private benefaction to budgeting. The diocese as a whole became responsible, the richer parishes giving of their 'abundance' to supply the 'necessity' of the poorer. It was, we said, bearing one another's burdens – the invidious word 'quota' was expunged – and it certainly helped to weld us into a family. Whatever our limitations in other ways, Southwell could claim to be at least a diocese, not a mere aggregate of parishes. I found some livings below subsistence level. Twenty years later more than half the benefices had been brought up to £1,200 or more and the average was well within sight of £1,000. Such figures are now no longer realistic, and are below many of those for unskilled labourers — but they were not too bad some twelve years ago.

One other small experiment from my early days may be of sufficient interest to mention. At St. John's, as I related in the previous chapter, we had tried to do something to help George Bell in rescuing victims of Hitler's persecution. Among those whom he had brought over there were some non-Aryan Lutheran pastors, precluded from the exercise of their ministry. Could they not be used, he was asking, in our own Church where we were so desperately short of clergy? Under persistent pressure from George, and with the consent of the Crown's legal advisers — for, as they were not British subjects, they could not take the oath of allegiance — I ordained two of these men to the priesthood and licensed them to curacies in the diocese. It was asking a good deal of a parish in the midst of the war to accept a German as curate. But, fine Christians as they were, they rose to it. There was no difficulty on this score, and little difficulty about language. What defeated us was Karl Barth's theology. The pure word as preached was totally incomprehensible to a middlebrow English congregation and no parish could stand it for very long at a time. One of them was an accomplished theologian, who is now well-known in ecumenical circles. When the war was over, the other went back to Germany to share in the rebuilding of his own Church. So there is at least one functioning Lutheran pastor who is an ordained priest of the Church of England.

I add here that, at a later stage of the war, we had a large camp of German prisoners, which in fact was more like a college than a prison. These were picked men who had been specially screened and were being trained to take part in the denazification of Germany. Educational courses were laid on for them, and, so far as security permitted, they were allowed to make local contacts. Some of these men were theological students, and

I had some instructive conversations with them. On one occasion, a kind of open day, I was invited to address the whole camp. There were a number of English visitors present, and at the end of the function the whole company joined together in saying the Lord's Prayer, "everyman in the tongue wherein he was born". It was a deeply moving experience and gave some ray of hope for the world's future. Even among all that strife and bitterness there was room for the word of reconciliation.

But in fact in this war there was nothing like the same amount of anti-German bitterness and hatred as had been so wickedly worked up during the first. Perhaps we had suffered too much for that. That was true at any rate in the early stages. When the people voted for the war they did not think they were fighting against 'Germany'. Rather they thought they were fighting to deliver it and the rest of mankind as well as themselves from a sterile tyranny and to save freedom for the world. But the most diabolical thing about total war is its septic corruption of motive. As it drags on feelings are hardened, bitterness and hatred increase and the war becomes its own justification. Till at last the 'unconditional surrender' formula, so ill thought out and so hastily adopted, made this a war of unlimited objective from which any negotiation was excluded.

Immeasurable damage resulted from it. In his speeches in the Lords and elsewhere George Bell had been strongly critical of this policy; and, in spite of all the abuse he received at the time, it is commonly recognised now that he was right. And this, not least by the military historians. "Hardly anyone would now question the wisdom of his repeated warnings about the folly of the Allies' unconditional surrender policy . . . Grand strategy looks beyond the war to the subsequent state of peace — and thus tends to coincide with morality. In this way, George Bell, standing for the principles of his creed, came to achieve a far clearer grasp of grand strategy than did the statesmen."[2]

When, almost by popular acclamation, Temple was called to succeed Lang at Canterbury, grief and dismay in the province

[2] Liddell Hart, quoted in Jasper's *George Bell*, p. 284.

of York were lightened by the thrill of expectancy with which both Church and nation looked forward to his leadership. Ought George Bell to have taken his place at York? As is now notorious, Churchill would have none of him because of his brave, persistent opposition to the policy of obliteration bombing, in which, again, he is seen now to have been right. That he should have been passed over remains a scandal. Yet it is not at all easy to be certain that he was entirely cut out for the primacy — he was, for one thing, a dreadfully dull speaker — or that he would not have been rather circumscribed by it.

But Cyril Garbett, who came against his own will — he was by now so deeply attached to Winchester — certainly made a great Archbishop of York; and as the years went on he was growing in stature, to become at the end a revered national figure. His appointment gave great pleasure to us personally. Since I first met him at Le Touquet my friendship with him had ripened and deepened and I had been admitted into his confidence. Before my own marriage I shared some holidays with him, one at the Lizard, another in Rome. He had frequently been in our home in Westminster and more than once we had stayed with him at Wolvesey. And, apart from my official visits to Bishopthorpe, we were now and again invited as guests. As my Metropolitan he was a tower of strength to me.

Neville Talbot and I went to his enthronement. As he entered the Minster in full regalia I happened to be on the steps, and as he passed he whispered, "Just had time to make the beds." Such was the environment of wartime primates. But can one imagine Lang ever saying that — or having the least idea how to make a bed?

I had only one serious disagreement with him, and that was about the rigoristic attitude which he took towards the question of marriage discipline. At the Lambeth Conference and in Convocation I tried in vain to resist an absolute rule forbidding remarriage in Church in all circumstances, with no power of discretion vested in anybody — as there is in the Episcopal Church of America. There are cases — everybody knows of them — in which the second marriage is the best chance of bringing people within the life of the Church and building up a true Christian home. It is not a question of fearing public opinion or of any meretricious desire to be hailed in the popular press as broadminded, but one of Christian appearances and realities. And it seemed to me that, as in some similar problems — 'indiscriminate baptism', for example — the harm that may be done by refusal can outweigh the good which it is hoped to realise. As a Bishop I was a man under authority and had to obey what the Church had ordered. I was not allowed to consider exceptional cases, and was bound to apply the rule as it stood. But, not seldom, I felt that I was doing wrong. It cheers me that now, even in higher echelons, the Church is having some second thoughts on this matter.

Shortly before D-day I had news that my father was nearing his end. Bournemouth, where he was, was then a prohibited area and I had to secure some kind of permit from the Lord Lieutenant (Lord Mottistone) to enter it. The Channel was already alive with shipping. As the invasion of Normandy moved forward, some streaks of dawn began to appear in our sky; we could dare to think about "the end of the war".

In July, I received a letter from William Temple, in which he asked me to lead a team of clergy including Milner White and Dwelly, to start work on the right form for a Victory service. With it he sent some notes to indicate the direction in which his own mind was moving.

I should like that at the central national service, after the King and Queen were seated, the choir should enter singing the *Miserere* in procession, omitting the last two verses, and that this should be followed by an Exhortation in which it was explained that at all times when our hearts are lifted up we should none the less approach God in penitence for our share in the whole sin of the world out of which come the calamities which afflict mankind, and that it should be as penitents that we offer our thanksgiving and our dedication which must always be the expression of our thanksgiving.

That, he recognised, might be too difficult for public opinion to stand or to understand. But he went on:

In its favour I may say that two years ago the Prime Minister asked me about using the word 'humiliation' in connexion with National Days of Prayer. He was strongly in favour of it, though he found that his colleagues differed from him. I told him that I did not want that word used till after we had won, but I should like it then. He was silent for a little while, and then said, "Yes, I understand that."

The full letter has since been printed by his nephew from the carbon copy at Lambeth.[3] But I quote this extract from it here because of the light which it throws on these two giants.

The letter was dated 12th July, 1944. He died on 25th October. By common consent, it was one of the worst disasters which has ever befallen the Church of England. I have recently paid my tribute to him elsewhere, on the twenty-fifth anniversary of his death.[4]

When the war in Europe finally came to its end and the Lord Mayor of Nottingham made the proclamation, I was with him on the balcony of the Council House. At his request I spoke through a microphone to the vast multitude in the Market Square "a word in the name of the Living God". There was an almost audible silence, cigarettes were put out, hats were lifted, and the crowd felt like a worshipping congregation. That scene has impressed itself on my memory. But I wonder, could it happen like that today? Or has the spirit of 'modern man' become so cheapened by commercialised entertainment as to have lost the capacity for reverence?

Partly to take my mind off the war, I had filled some of the long black-out evenings putting down some thoughts about the

[3] *Some Lambeth Letters, 1942–1944*, ed. F. S. Temple (OUP, 1963), pp. 175, 176

[4] *New Christian*, 16th October 1969.

Church and its post-war mission to the nation, which were published under the title *Church and Leadership*. This sold out quickly, but it was not reprinted. Much of it was, no doubt, ephemeral stuff; and the whole situation to which it was addressed has now become radically different from anything that we could have foreseen — or at any rate, did foresee — at the time.

2 SPRING

Shortages and restrictions continued, and indeed in the first post-war years they were worse than they had been during the war itself. But the darkness was past; the lifting of the blackout seemed to be the symbol of a new dawn. As after the first war, so now, we believed that a better world was within our reach. We had failed before, but we would not fail now. If the League of Nations had broken down, then the United Nations this time would be 'different'. If our social order was still so full of wrongs, this time we would not fail in righting them. No doubt we shared the pathetic human delusion that because we had been through such unspeakable horrors, everything *must* now move away from them. The consoling dogma of automatic progress was killed dead by the news of Hiroshima — a stunning shock to public opinion, which now had to realise that we were moving, not into an age of effortless security, but into one of new and appalling danger in which the whole human race might be destroyed. The fight against the "world rulers of this darkness" was more than one against Hitler and Mussolini. In that fight did man stand alone in a neutral or even hostile universe? It is the fear or belief that this is the truth which is gnawing the heart of post-war society.

The war could not have been won without America; but it was this country which had borne the brunt of it, standing alone with the Commonwealth in its finest hour. Britain might have exhausted itself materially, but it held a unique place of moral authority, which the world was looking to it to exercise.

Had it the moral and spiritual resources? The Church had stood by the people in the evil day. William Temple had re-created its image and through him it had held the confidence of the millions; and even though now deprived of Temple it had a unique opportunity of leadership, in the reawakening of a living faith and in helping to rebuild national life. Would it be rebuilt on Christian foundations or would it "go a-whoring after other gods"? The Church had its chance if it knew how to take it.

"A lead from the Church" has now become rather a cliché, and means in effect a speech by an Archbishop. Yet perhaps it is not totally mistaken. Granted that the Church is not the clergy and that if it 'leads' it leads through its members in their manifold secular occupations, it remains true that the vitality of its members is largely evoked by a lead from above. Whatever its theological justification, the real pragmatic argument for episcopacy rests, not on appeal to its record (for on that evidence how can it be defended?), but on the opportunity it provides for a personal initiative and leadership. And as life began to open up again my own history moved into a period of full and varied episcopal activity.

Demobilisation was only just beginning and most of the forces were still overseas. Archbishop Fisher arranged that the Bishops should go out in succession to visit them and take them a message from the Church at home. When my own turn came I was sent to the army of occupation in Germany. Of course they gave me a thoroughly good time, but it was, all the same, a harrowing experience. One had the chance of fairly close contact with the military occupation authorities, gallantly attempting whatever was in their power — and admittedly making some dreadful mistakes in the process — to cope with the appalling situation of hunger and helplessness in the German people. I saw what had been done to the Ruhr and Hamburg. I was able to talk with some of the Lutheran pastors and a group of theological professors — though starving men are not open to rational argument; and all I heard, from British as well as

German sources, left me with an increasingly troubled conscience. Some of the things which appeared to be being mishandled came to be rectified as time went on and civilian experts were brought in to advise in a task almost beyond human power.

But my primary mission was to the British forces. This involved the familiar routine of addresses and confirmations in various centres. But it also provided opportunities of conversation with officers and men, and learning what they wanted to see when they came home and what they hoped the Church would do. And perhaps the most valuable part, for me, was the time spent in meeting the chaplains — browned-off and hypercritical of authority, much as we had been twenty-five years before — and hearing from them what they had learnt, what were their hopes and visions for the Church, and trying to understand their complaints and grievances. I came back a 'fuller' man than I had gone out.

The chaplains were now beginning to return, some to the benefices that they had left, others to livings that had been kept vacant for them, so that we could begin again to staff the parishes, and many in which Church life had inevitably been at a low ebb began to revive. But we were desperately short of manpower. The Church had been offered exemption for its candidates, like the medical profession, but had decided to keep back nothing from the national effort. Consequently, during the war there had been the merest trickle of ordinations and the natural wastage through death or retirement was nothing like replaced by new intake. The total number of clergy available was short, by some thousands, of its pre-war strength. The problem was primarily one of curates. But even for finding incumbents for the parishes there were not nearly enough men to go round, and the Church was faced with a major crisis which endangered the whole parochial system. After the first war it had been saved by Knutsford. This time it was saved, but only just, by a radical rearrangement of the system. The cynic might say that it was by falling back on the eighteenth century abuses of pluralities and non-residence; for it meant a drastic redeployment of manpower and a large-scale combination of parishes in the thinly populated rural areas.

My grandfather was for twenty years rector of a hamlet in the Norfolk broadland (Fishley, near Acle Bridge) of which the total population including the rectory household, numbered eighteen! That particular case may have been indefensible. But it was an exaggeration of a principle which is one of the secrets of our history and a great part of the strength of the Church of England — the resident priest in every community. The question was not so much what he *did*, how many man-hours he clocked up per week. What was required of him was that he should *reside*, should be there, sharing the life of his parishioners and identified with that community — and that has stood for something far more than statistical calculations can ever measure. But there simply were not the men enough for that now. The parochial system could only be saved now by a fairly drastic redistribution. Even had the men been available to put a whole-time priest into every village, not many villages could have found the money to make the nominal 'living' a livelihood.

I could never have agreed to any policy of starving the country in order to feed the town. That had been the mistake of nineteenth-century governments and, to some extent, of the nineteenth-century Church, which had tended at least to suggest that 'good men' ought not to be wasted on country parishes — where, in fact, there are the greatest opportunities. But for the sake of the villages themselves, to provide them with a ministry at all, there had to be some rationalisation. Two or even three little parishes had to be united to form a single benefice, and sharing one rector between them. This, of course, is always unpopular — and, for myself, I thanked God that it was, for it showed how much the clergy had done for the people. It would almost never be willingly accepted. There would always be reasons why this particular parish could not possibly unite with that. One of the strangest arguments I remember was that "We were on different sides during the war" — the war having been that between King and Parliament. But slowly and steadily during the post-war years this measure of pastoral reorganisation, "to make better provision for the cure of souls", was put into operation in all the dioceses. In Southwell it did not have to be half so drastic as in the devastated urban dioceses, and at first we were mainly concerned with the rural areas. Something was lost that can never be recovered. But the Bishop of Taunton has argued that, on balance, the country parishes gained more than they lost, since now that they could offer a man-sized job and something more like a man-sized income, they could command the service of better men. In the past too many of the little Fishleys had been held by men of slender qualifications who had given up hope of preferment elsewhere, except, perhaps, cemetery chaplaincies.[5]

In addition to this, all through the war years the machinery had been running in bottom gear. No repairs had been possible to the churches, parsonage houses had to be left untouched and some had now become almost uninhabitable, and the state of many Church schools was a scandal. All these accumulated arrears of work had now to be tackled — and somehow or other paid for. And, as Government housing plans developed, new estates were springing up in all directions, which must all be provided with churches and vicarages. All this entailed, among other things, the financial restructuring of the diocese and the raising of large sums of new money. Thus the next ten years were to be in every way a time of reconstruction and rebuilding. It was a hard job but it was exhilarating. As the world moved into a new stage of history, we were trying to see to it that the Church did not stay behind, but took its rightful place. We were looking to the future and in hope.

But the danger was to become so absorbed in repairing and retooling the machinery as to forget what mattered far more

[5] See Frank West, *The Country Parish Today and Tomorrow* (SPCK), pp. 28–46.

than that. If the Church was to be the leader of national life, and to give moral and religious guidance in the building of a new social order, better organisation was not enough. Better organisation is important, but is of strictly secondary importance. The question is, what are we organising *for*? It is implied in the principle of stewardship that the Church should make the best use of its resources; so that bad accounting or waste can be sinful. But is it using them just to stay in being, or to discharge its mission more effectively? It has been a tragedy that now as then the Church has allowed itself to become bogged down in the secondary administrative problems and preoccupied with its own internal politics, too prone to follow the line of least resistance and evade the primary, fundamental questions, which are socio-ethical and theological.

So, as in one small diocese we set out to rebuild the external life of the Church, we must try not to neglect what mattered far more — its own interior spiritual vitality. And, humanly speaking at least, that depended, and could not but depend, on the leadership. But, as an executive ought not to type the letters, so a Church leader is likely to fail to lead if he lets himself be immersed in minor details.[6] Amid the rising tide of committee work which the diocesan enterprise involved, could the Bishop keep his own head above water?

The answer to that lay with his generous colleagues, who took most of the burden on to their own shoulders. I rather

---

[6] I had learnt that lesson, like many others, early in life from Archbishop Davidson. When I was Principal of Knutsford, I had gone to him with Guy Vernon Smith (afterwards Bishop of Leicester) to ask for his ruling or advice on a tangle of internal problems. "I should have gone mad years ago," he said, "if I had attended to little things like that. I gave you a major policy decision. You men must implement it in its details." I know, of course, that some outstanding bishops, such as Mervyn Haigh and Lord Fisher — and George Bell would probably have agreed with them — would differ strongly from what I have said in the text, pointing out how often grand strategy can break down through neglect of some minor detail. ("For want of a nail a shoe was lost . . .") I only query whether this is the bishop's job — any more than it is the general's job. In the end, no doubt, every man will do his best work by following his own particular bent.

enjoy organising things; it is much less tiring than personal interviews or preparing a sermon or trying to write an article. But I never would claim to have been a 'good administrator', and at raising money I was no good at all. If the diocese was well administered — as other people, apparently, thought it was — that was not really due to myself; it was because we worked as a team. I should loathe to seem to be telling a cheap success-story. God knows, I make no claims to have 'succeeded'; I am far too well aware of the limitations. Yet it would be mock-humility to suggest that my time at Southwell had been a total failure. But honour where honour is due — if anything got done during my episcopate it was due to the fact that so many others were willing to share with me in a common task. And I do not doubt that one of the rules of leadership is the delega-tion of responsibility, the whole way down through the structure of authority. If people are always waiting to be 'told' what they ought to do, initiative is stifled, and too much potential energy runs to waste. It was this belief, whatever it may be worth, that we tried to put into practice at Southwell.

No Bishop could have had an abler or more devoted diocesan staff than mine; and we worked together in trust and under-standing. I can hardly express what I owe to the archdeacons, who tended, too soon, to be moved to higher office. When Victor Turner left us for Penrith, Roger Wilson, who had been with me at St. John's and had meantime been Vicar of Blackpool, rejoined me as Archdeacon of Nottingham. When he was whisked away to be Bishop of Wakefield, I persuaded the Secretary of CACTM, John Phillips, to come and take his place. A few years later, on a Christmas morning, just as I was going into the Minster, John was on the telephone to tell me that he had been offered the bishopric of Portsmouth: I have seldom preached a worse Christmas sermon. Once again I had recourse to CACTM and Michael Brown accepted the archdeaconry. After the resignation of Percy Hales, Frank West joined me as Archdeacon of Newark, and quickly showed that he had a touch of genius for the work that fell to him in the rural areas. When, towards the end of my time, he published his book on the country parish, he became widely known in the Church at large, and was soon claimed for the Bishopric of Taunton. The present Bishop of Sherwood succeeded him. Thus I enjoyed a succession of brilliant colleagues, and no diocese could have been better served.

The conventional image of an archdeacon suggests a stiff and hardhearted official prying into clerical shortcomings. But he is, or can be, the parson's best friend, and essentially his office is pastoral. Even his statutory and legal duties, such as looking after parsonage houses, are concerned rather with people than regulations. And within his area he exercises a large measure of delegated *episcope* for the general wellbeing of the Church. The same applies also to the rural dean. Instead of diminishing bishops into rural deans, which seems to be now the fashionable prescription, it is better to magnify rural deans to a status approaching that of local *episcopoi*, trusted with a responsible autonomy in the administration of their deaneries, in accordance with agreed diocesan policy.

Not least, it applies to the incumbents. The chief object of the whole exercise is to sustain the morale of the clergy and evoke from them the best that they have to give. If I learnt anything as a Bishop it was that the man who matters most in the Ministry is the parish priest on the spot. All administration, or new legislation, should be directed to strengthening his position and encouraging his responsible independence. Any schemes which tend to undermine that will change the character of the Church of England and immeasurably weaken its influence. That, at least, is the lesson of my own small experience.

Gradually this sense of responsibility began to make itself felt in the life of the diocese. The clergy began to think more about the Church than about their sectional allegiances and to outgrow their suspicions of authority. Parishes began to emerge from parochially minded isolationism. And before too long there were signs of a changed attitude in the meetings of the

Diocesan Conference. During my first few years I had dreaded these functions, which were too often factious and unpleasant, firing hostile questions at the platform and apparently anxious to defeat the government. The 'We' and 'They' syndrome was endemic. One could hear people saying, as they left the hall, "I don't in the least agree with that decision and have no intention of carrying it out, but one cannot openly vote against the Bishop". It took a lot of patient explanation to get them to understand that they were not voting either for the Bishop or against him, but for or against proposals introduced by their own elected representatives — the diocesan board of finance, for example. (The annual budget was not the Bishop's budget about which he was "determined to get his own way".) By the end of my time I had come to enjoy these meetings, at which people, who now trusted one another and understood what the diocese was about, came together as friends to debate and make decisions in a spirit of corporate responsibility. (There are now to be no more diocesan Conferences!)

But the diocese could not have functioned at all without the successive diocesan secretaries, Canon Lee, Colonel Mitchell and after him Mr. Hyde, who inspired confidence throughout the parishes, and the skilled secretariat at Church House. A word of appreciation is due to them, as well as to my two legal secretaries, first Noel Parr and after him Richard Beaumont, who guided me through the mysteries of Church law.

There is all the difference in the world between being Bishop *of* and Bishop *in*. English dioceses are territorial and mine coincided with the county boundaries. So I tried hard to be Bishop of Nottinghamshire, not only of Anglican churchmen who lived in it. This involved spending much time and energy — there were critics who said, too much of both — in extra-ecclesiastical activities, in frequent visits to factories and coal pits and in numerous civic and academic functions which were the symbolic expressions of public life. These, it could be

argued, had "nothing to do with the Church"; and if it is the
chief function of the clergy to increase the number of people at
church services, there was often admittedly little enough
'result' from them. But at least they provided a 'presence' of
the Church identified with the life of the community, and they
frequently led to important pastoral contacts. In England, for
many reasons — some the wrong reasons — a diocesan Bishop
can sometimes have access to places and human situations
which the parish priest finds it hard to enter. Is it then merely
'worldly' or waste of time if he tries to buy up those opportunities? And often, before he leaves, it has been possible to
open a door for the parish priest to follow.

And naturally I gave as much time as I could to the schools —
not only, of course the Church schools — and the various centres
of higher education. Thus I tried to secure the confidence of the
teaching profession and to give what backing I could to the
teachers. In the schools of today teachers who are Christians
are in the very front line of the Church's ministry, and deserve,
and need, far more support and help from the Church than is
always given them. We were able later to build up weekend
courses for them, which led on, in time, to systematic conferences between the clergy and local welfare workers; and
the diocese enjoyed very friendly and trustful relations with
the local education authorities, something which does not
happen automatically and was due very largely to our Director
of Education, Eric Roberts. If the Church gives the unfortunate
impression of being mainly concerned about its 'rights', the
authorities will meet it on the same terms. It must show that it
really cares about education.

Yet a Bishop's primary obligation is to be Father-in-God to
his own people and particularly, above all else, to be *pastor
pastorum* to his fellow clergy. From the Lord Lieutenant, the
Duke of Portland, downwards, the laymen had rallied round
me right from the start. The clergy, or some of them, were a bit
suspicious — a 'liberal' Bishop is likely to be suspect. As their
worst fears proved to be unrealised they were generously

willing to trust me, and we soon became a closely united brother-hood, walking in the house of God as friends. When I was recently asked what, in my opinion, is the most important part of the Bishop's job, my reply was, "Having tea in the vicarages"; and, in principle, I meant it quite seriously. The parson's home is an integral part of his ministry, and the Bishop ought, as far as he may, to be known in it; few things can do more to streng-then the bond of unity between him and his colleagues than tea with the vicarage family.

For some years on end the munificence of a layman made it possible for us to take the clergy, with their wives and their little ones and their household gods, for a mid-week holiday in a Butlin's camp, and it paid rich spiritual dividends. And of course we did our best to make Bishop's Manor a home for the clergy and the whole diocese. If there was any 'success' in my episcopate, it was largely due to the personal trust and friendship which the Southwell clergy allowed me to share with them, and for which I can never be sufficiently grateful.

This may be the place to mention something which cannot be left out of a truthful record. As my friends and my family know only too well, I have been dogged through most of my working life by an inherited tendency to deafness, which, as only the deaf can understand, doubles the strain of every under-taking and frequently leaves one nervously exhausted. I was not born deaf. Although as a little child I suffered from ex-cruciating ear-aches, about which too little was known so long ago — the cure for ear-ache then was castor oil — it was not until my early manhood that I began to be consciously hard of hearing. This, as happened to many other people, was accen-tuated during the first war by the vibrations of heavy guns and shell fire, and after that the condition began to deteriorate. When I went to Southwell I could still manage quite well, though I had, before long, to have recourse to an aid; and with the most delicate tact and kindness, people helped me in every possible way, so that I was never totally incapacitated.

But such troubles do not improve as a man grows older, and the time came at last when I was no longer able to hear what was being said in a committee or to take the chair at a public meeting. Then was the time to withdraw into private life. But I know very well how heavy a demand this affliction has made on those around me and indeed on all those to whom I have tried to minister, and what patient understanding they have given me. If this disability has been overcome, it is as much by others as by myself.

A great part of any Bishop's work is of course defined for him in advance by the functions inherent in his office. In a sense, all Bishops must always be doing the same things — confirmations, ordinations, institutions, consecrating new churches and burial grounds (on these latter occasions it seemed to be always snowing). To these must be added, so far as is humanly possible, celebrating and preaching in the parishes. In this routine of liturgical activities, it is confirmations that are most apparent, and are what a Bishop is commonly thought to be *for*. It may well seem, no doubt, to any onlooker that this is an easy enough thing to do, but I found it, myself, one of the most difficult, and my first untried attempts were calamitous. Slowly one learns by experience how to do it, though I am not at all sure that I know yet. Because one has to do it so often, it can become a kind of conditioned reflex. It is fatally easy, if one is not careful, to take the whole service, including the address, while thinking all the time about something else. To resist that routinisation, to remain vital and spiritually sensitive, and to make the service something very special for the candidates and, not least, for their parents — all this is likely to take a good deal out of a man.

The post-confirmation wastage is notorious. Not more than a third of those confirmed seem to remain as regular communicants. One reason for that may be lack of support at home. But there is, I think, another which goes deep into the whole nature and meaning of confirmation. Surely it is the sacrament of growth, and is best approached as a *rite de passage* — the Christian version of tribal puberty rituals. Baptism is about being born. Confirmation is about growing up, in human development and in the Christian life — "daily increasing in the Holy Spirit". Too often boys and girls take the line that once confirmed they have "finished with religion". They have graduated out of the junior class now, and have, as it were, passed the examination. They can leave religion behind now with childhood. But the emphasis ought to be the exact opposite, moving forward into adult life, accepting new Christian responsibilities, learning more advanced Christian lessons, empowered by grace for becoming a grown-up person. If this is true, then the welcome and encouragement and the training given after confirmation matter more than the *ad hoc* preparation for it. And about seventeen is probably the 'best' age.

From the first, my annual programme of confirmations was lightened by the help of assistant bishops. After Neville's death, Douglas Wilson of Honduras (now Canon of Wells) shared the episcopal work with me for some years. After him we secured that gallant man John Weller, retired from his arduous diocese in the Falkland Islands, who was in all sorts of ways a strong support to me. In my later years I had as colleagues Mark Way (formerly Bishop of Masasi) and Bishop Gwynne's successor in the Sudan, Morris Gelsthorpe, of whom I have more to say later. And it certainly brought an enrichment to the diocese to have these bishops from overseas around in it.

But the institutions I always did myself. These give invaluable opportunity for coming into close touch with a parish, introducing their new incumbent to them, offering them encouragement and counsel, and meeting the general body of parishioners at the party in the church hall which follows. The latter is an important part of the function, and the Bishop loses a great deal if he cuts it, however weary (or hungry!) he may be feeling. But for a Bishop to take an institution happily and confidently there is one condition: he must honestly believe that the incumbent whom he is instituting is the right man. That raises the

whole question of patronage, about which I shall try to say
something in the last chapter.

The highlights, of course, were the ordinations – the Bishop's
highest and most responsible privilege – for, whatever his
advisers may advise, it is he alone who can and must decide
whether a man is to be ordained or not – and the time when, if
ever in his ministry, he is Father-in-God to his spiritual sons.
These are the happiest times in the annual round; and the
ordinations are what I now chiefly miss. I must have ordained
some 250 – if not more – men into the Anglican ministry. With
some of them I am still able to keep in touch. Some now occupy
prominent positions and I am proud to have started them on
their way. But now that one reads announcements in the Church
press that men whom I had ordained are about to retire, it
makes me feel like a latter-day Methuselah.

English Bishops, Davidson used to insist, are Bishops of
England, not only of their dioceses, and incur much extra-
diocesan work. In addition to Convocation and Church
Assembly and, when they reach it, the House of Lords, most
of them will be chairmen or members of one or more central
committees and boards. They are therefore obliged to be
frequently in London.

Northern Convocation, of course, meets in York. Even if the
agenda was sometimes rather trivial, it was always an enjoyable
occasion. The bishops were invited to stay at Bishopthorpe.
(During the period of food rationing we had to arrive with
little screws of butter and tea and sugar and bacon in our robe
cases; but Frances Temple, and Elsie Garbett after her, always
managed to give us a fine dinner.) Moreover, the Convocation
of York was small enough for most of the members to know
one another, and the two Houses normally sat together, so that
it felt like a meeting of personal friends.

During my time the Upper House was a strong team. After
the President, the ablest man in the Northern Province was
Williams of Carlisle, one of Lloyd George's early nominations.
The selection caused a little surprise at the time, but it was in

fact a thoroughly good appointment. With his wise judgement and powerful intellect he brought great strength to the bench, and in his diocese he was a greatly beloved pastoral Bishop. There were also Alwyn Williams at Durham, Leslie Hunter at Sheffield, Crick at Chester, Guy Warman at Manchester and others of distinguished ability. Their successors in the next generation were undoubtedly strong and able men. It is certainly not true that the Bishops of the Northern Province were a second eleven. I spoke when I had anything to say, mainly on educational subjects and on the selection and training of the clergy. The debates were often on a high level; but it vexed me that, in the one place where it could have been done, so little time was given to the great moral and theological questions and so much to the revision of canons and other matters of internal politics. Even debates of the House of Lords type could have done so much to lead Church opinion.

If the Church Assembly has not achieved what the sponsors of the Enabling Act had hoped from it, one has to admit that probably it could not. It is primarily a legislative body and must therefore be mainly occupied with the day to day business of running the Church in a constantly changing situation. Yet should it not debate ends as well as means? Over the years I made a few fighting speeches and was now and again received with some enthusiasm. But I found these meetings a weariness to the flesh.

The House of Lords is a nearly absolute contrast. It could truly be said that a Bishop's chance of 'counting' in it depends on his understanding of the difference. It is not an ecclesiastical assembly and any approach to preaching would be insufferable. He must respect the House for what it is, in its rightful and inherent laicity. The Bishops are there as part of the constitution and their function is to interpret Christian principle in secular social and political questions, not only in those which directly concern the Church – the Church is concerned with all matters of human welfare. But they have to *know* what they are talking about. This is no place for amateurish 'idealism'. One's maiden speech is a most alarming ordeal, but after that one begins to pluck up courage. There is probably no Chamber in the world that commands such a wealth of expert knowledge or so rich a variety of experience, and I found their Lordships' House altogether fascinating.

The 1948 Lambeth Conference, brilliantly chaired by Geoffrey Fisher who, in common with most of the others present, had never himself taken part in one, has been sufficiently described in other books. It was speaking in and to a situation which already belongs to past history, and can only be fairly assessed in that context. What fundamentally mattered was that it met. The Japanese Bishops, for example, had come out of the great tribulation and were now to confer with Americans for the first time. Indian Bishops were meeting British. Gulfs of tension and bitterness were transcended in the unity of faith and fellowship, so that there was given to us wider vision of the worldwide Anglican communion and its ministry of reconciliation.

The report on the Christian doctrine of Man, most of which, as it happened, I wrote myself, has been criticised as unsatisfactory. So it is, twenty or more years later, in a radically changed context. The strongly humanist tone of the report must be understood against the background of the "savage and inhuman theologies" of the then dominant 'neo-orthodoxy'. I do not think it was too bad at the time, and it received quite a warm welcome. But I should agree with Canon Purcell's criticism.[7] The Church's task today, as never before, is to vindicate the humanity of man against all that is threatening to dehumanise us. But the whole situation has changed since then; and if I were asked now to draft a document on Christian anthropology in the present context, it would have to be written in very different terms. In an *ad hoc* book, *The Recovery of Man*, I tried to provide some background material for the Lambeth report and to commend it.

That conference brought me a number of new friendships

[7] *Fisher of Lambeth*, p. 182.

among Anglican Bishops in other parts of the world, and not
least in the United States, which were to lead in due course to
extensive travels.

There were still to be many years of full work, both within
the diocese and beyond it, and the further a man moves forward
into his ministry the more and the more demanding become its
claims upon him. The greater, therefore, his danger of running
dry and becoming routinised rather than creative.

A Bishop has to be constantly giving out, with too little
opportunity for quiet and keeping himself spiritually alive. He
may too easily cease to be a leader and content himself with
seeing that the machine continues to run—or "stopping it
from stopping". It is not nearly so simple a matter as compulsory
retirement at sixty. A man should be at his peak at sixty-five,
and many men are doing their best work—Cyril Garbett was
one of the classical instances—between seventy and seventy-
five, or later. (Archbishop Frederick Temple had been eighty
when he was *appointed* to Canterbury, though I should not wish
to suggest that as a precedent.)

By this time I was in my fifty-ninth year and approaching
the middle-aged period of my ministry, and in need of some
relaxation and refuelling. So when I had completed ten years at
Southwell I asked to be granted a sabbatical term. And—
largely, I think, on George Bell's initiative—I received from
Bishop Sherril, the presiding Bishop, whom I had got to know
well at Lambeth, an invitation to pay a three months' visit,
with Lilian, as the guests of the Protestant Episcopal Church of
the USA (PECUSA). It happened that Rosemary had just
left school, having secured her entrance to Cambridge, and
with characteristic American generosity she was included in the
invitation. Of course it would mean a great deal of preaching and
lecturing; it was not what everybody would call a holiday. But it
could not fail to be immensely stimulating. So in February
1952 we three set out together from Liverpool.

The arrangements had been worked out by Lawrence Rose,

Dean of the General Theological Seminary, and friend of so many English parsons visiting New York. (A few years later he came over here and I took him to see the minster in old York.) They began with a Lent course in the seminary. During the first six or eight weeks, therefore, we were based on New York itself, housed in an apartment near Chelsea Square. I preached week by week in the college chapel and enjoyed close contact with staff and students. In the intervals, and at week-ends, I was engaged elsewhere in the city, where I spoke in some of the metropolitan churches, taking a course in Holy Trinity, Wall Street, or in other States within easy reach. Just before we left England in February the beloved King George VI had died, and I was able to offer a word of thanks, as a representative of the Church of England, for the moving and spontaneous tributes which the American people had offered to him. I spoke to clergy in Newark, New Jersey (the original Newark is in the Southwell diocese) and preached or lectured in Philadelphia, in Boston (in Philip Brooks' pulpit), as well as in various places in Connecticut with a long weekend in Washington, DC, where I functioned in St. John's, Lafayette Square, and in other centres, too numerous to retail. I spoke in a number of universities, Columbia, Yale, Harvard and others and in the Divinity School at Cambridge, Massachusetts. And it inflates any man's ego to be invited to dine with the Fellows of Harvard, who are probably the most distinguished academic common room in the world. Whenever we were in New York and free, I would walk long distances in Central Park, and the Roses were anxious about my health — or sanity. (When I once told my hosts in Connecticut that I needed a couple of hours to walk, they thought it so hazardous an undertaking that they had the car follow me the whole way.)

Lilian had some engagements on her own account. She had been very active in the diocese, amongst other ways, in the clubs and hostels run by the Girls' Friendly Society, of which, in this year, she became central president — an exacting post, involving much travelling and administrative work — which she held almost up to the time of my retirement. The American GFS was at that time highly developed, and as representing the parent society she was asked to a number of conferences and like functions. When she was away, Rosemary went around with me, and we went down together to Tennessee, where I gave a number of lectures and addresses in the University of the South, a foundation of the Episcopal Church, which had been set up after the Civil War through the efforts of a wellknown theologian, Du Bose, who had been one of the Confederate generals. This was my first contact with the deep South, and in those few days one learned a great deal! After Holy Week addresses in New York, we spent Easter at two of the best known private schools, Hotchkiss and Kent. After that we were sent further afield. But before we left, the seminary conferred on me the honour of its STP degree.

Then began a long and exciting journey, to the Middle West, Chicago and Evanston (where I gave some addresses in the seminary) to Kansas City ('the real America'), where I preached in the cathedral and spoke to clergy, thence by devious routes into Arizona, where we had a long day at the Grand Canyon, and at last across the desert to San Francisco. It was one of the dreams of my life come true when like stout Cortes we gazed on the Pacific. Seldom have I enjoyed anything so much as the week we spent in San Francisco, where, when I was not officially occupied, the Bishop took us on wonderful expeditions, through the Redwood forests or to the diocesan ranch. Thence by rail across Oregon to Seattle, where Stephen Bayne, Bishop of Olympia, had laid on a full programme of engagements, a clergy school and talks of many other kinds. But we had a day with him in the Olympic mountains (from which the diocese takes its strange name) and the Admiral lent us his launch to tour the harbour. We could not possibly have been made more welcome and I still remember that week with delight.

We were to travel home by way of Canada. So Stephen took us across Puget Sound and handed us over at Vancouver to

Godfrey Gower, Bishop of New Westminster (now Archbishop of Columbia), with whom I formed a close and lasting friendship. There were many engagements in that lovely city and plenty of new knowledge to be lapped up. We had a few days at Victoria, Vancouver Island (more Victorian English than England), as the guests of Archbishop Sexton, and by now the time had come to turn east again.

The transcontinental journey was entrancing, as the train climbs up through the Rockies to the Great Divide, then down through Alberta across the endless prairies, and on through the Ontario lakes and forests — a world of seemingly infinite space. We stopped off at Banff, for a few days' holiday, walking in the mountains among the black bears, and of course visiting Lake Louise, kept a few appointments in Toronto (of which I was to see much more later on), thence to Quebec and across to Liverpool. We caught the Mersey tide and the train to Euston, and appeared that evening at the Lord Mayor's banquet as though we had never been away at all.

We both have a passion for going places, but we had gone enough for the time being. It had been altogether a wonderful three months, full of new, enlarging experiences, with many new friendships cemented and with memories to last a lifetime, and we came back stimulated and refreshed. Bishop Weller and the two archdeacons had looked after the diocese so well that it had taken no harm through my absence. Indeed, it seemed to have got on rather better. I hoped to serve it now with renewed vigour.

3 SUMMER

In one sense it is true that 'our church' and 'our vicar' is the strength and the secret of the Church of England. To most of its members it is what the Church means. It subsists in its local embodiments and loyalties, so that the strength or weakness of its influence always has been, and probably always will be, the strength or weakness of its parochial life. The proposals which seem now to be fashionable to streamline, or abolish, all local

organisations and substitute membership in 'the Church' —
an idea far too remote and generalised to mean anything very
concrete in particular — surely rests on a quite false psychology.
So a bishop must always do everything he can to support and
deepen the church life of the parishes, for it is by this that the
'ordinary chap' is sustained in Christian faith and living.

On the other hand 'my parish' can be the devil, keeping the
parson in blinkers and like the old horse that went round and
round driving a primitive engine. And, by the same token, 'our
church' can symbolise a petty parochialism which even resents
'outsiders' coming in, and tends to regard the Church as little
more than a club for 'good' and religiously minded people.
There were plenty of them about in the ancient world. Was
Calvary endured just for that? What it comes to is that churchmen are always in danger of thinking about the Church of
God as something that we possess, that belongs to us, rather
than as something that claims us for ends and purposes greater
than itself. Christ is for all men, not for believers only.

So I was always trying to teach the parishes to look out
beyond the self-enclosed churchy world and to find their
mission and ministry within, and not merely alongside, the
common life. I would say, indeed, that my whole life and
ministry, whether in writing, preaching or other ways, has been
an attempt to carry the Christian faith beyond the circle of
professed believers to those who are on the fringes of Christianity
and too often separated from it by walls of ignorance and mis-
understanding. And although the theological explosion of the
sixties was still in the future and unforeseen, it was already clear
that the Church was faced with a major crisis of belief. I
constantly tried to put it to my fellow bishops that this was the
central question before the Church. But, then as now, it was
weakened by the lack of brave, informed theological leadership.

But how could I, as diocesan, reach the fringes and speak to
those who would not be there to listen to me? When I first
arrived everything I said got headlines in the local press —
and a very good, independent press it was; but as I grew older

At the Southwell Millenary, 1956.

Visiting a coal pit, 1950.

(*top*) My first grandchild's first Christmas, 1960.

At The Coppice, three generations, 1968.

Ourselves, Grindelwald, 1968.

and was no longer new, my news value perceptibly diminished. So, as at St. John's, I fell back on my own journalism.

Every diocese runs a monthly leaflet, with a circulation of 30,000 or more, and often passed from one household to another. containing a message or letter from the Bishop. This is his main channel of communication. If he just jots down a few pious sentiments, or attempts (as instructed from above) to sell the latest stunt in ecclesiastical politics – such as some complex Church Assembly measure – few really 'lay' laymen will pay much attention. But it can be used for more important purposes. I took immense trouble with these letters, claiming two large-type pages out of the four, and trying month by month to expound some fundamental doctrine of Christianity which might be currently misunderstood – and in this I was sometimes helpfully coached by the Provost, whose scholarship was far better than mine – or to offer an approach to a Christian judgement on some moral or social problem under debate. These letters were read far beyond the diocese and were sometimes given a quote in the national press or reproduced in other Church publications. And though, of course, they varied in quality – the divine afflatus cannot be had to order – I think they did make a certain impact.

But my more ambitious experiment was a failure. Soon after returning from North America I decided to launch the *Southwell Review* – a very well printed and well produced quarterly containing most of the features of its kind, local history and archaeology, studies of Nottinghamshire industries, prospects of the Notts XI, personal reminiscences, books, the arts, the cinema – the lot. I wrote the leaders, which were theological, and sometimes contributed a signed article. Here, I hoped, was a symbol of what we were getting at, and a manifesto of Christian humanism – *nihil humani alienum*. It did very well. It went all over the world. Distinguished people were kindly willing to write for it and it attracted favourable notice. But within the diocese it was a total flop and was almost boycotted by the clergy. They declared that it served no useful purpose (there were no little churchy odds and ends in it). The *Review* lasted for five or six years, after which, to my disappointment, the diocese withdrew its small subsidy. They were hitting me rather harder than they realised.

So far as concerned the clergy more directly, the main focus of educational effort was the annual autumn conference at Swanwick, at which we tried to think theologically about our personal and pastoral problems. Normally we had a visiting speaker, though now and again I did the whole thing myself. But I always had two or three sessions with them, at which I said whatever I wanted to say and answered questions in free-for-all debate. Here one could speak freely and uninhibitedly, and allow oneself an occasional indiscretion, by way of offering them some new idea or inserting into their thinking a doubt or two about some conventional established judgements. I was, so they said, at my best on these occasions. The Swanwicks were certainly some of my happiest times; and these days together, away from the parishes, in an atmosphere of friendship and trust, did a great deal to weld us into a brotherhood.

We took great pains with post-ordination training, where we had the help of Nottingham university. (I do not quite understand why CACTM now wants to get all this into its own clutches instead of supporting diocesan initiative.) One archdeacon spent nearly half his time in keeping in touch with the newly ordained men, seeing them twice a year in their own homes. And we encouraged the ruri-decanal chapters to spend their meetings in studying a book together; I tried myself to spend a morning with each of them once a year to join in their discussions and attempt to handle their theological difficulties.

It may not have added up to very much, but it was about as much as could be done in a diocese with no canon theologian.

At the Coronation in 1953 all the Bishops and their wives were summoned. At George VI's Coronation I had been present as one of the canons of Westminster and as such had carried the Bible in the procession of the Regalia. This time I was but a privileged spectator. It was moving and magnificent beyond belief. Queen and Archbishop did their part superbly, and it made a profound impression on the nation who could now, for the first time, watch it in their own homes. This is one of the memories that remain through life. Was it the last? I shall never know whether my grandchildren have witnessed the Coronation of Charles III.

Two years later we welcomed Her Majesty when she came to the Royal Show at Nottingham — a day crowded with ceremonial functions. By her own wish, she and Prince Philip spent an hour with us at the Church building, and her gracious act did a power of good. Despite chronology, this is the natural place to refer to another notable royal visit. One of the major occasions in the diocese was the millenary of Southwell minster in 1956 and we tried to celebrate this on a fitting scale. Princess Margaret accepted my invitation to be present at the great service in the minster, at which the Archbishop of York, then Michael Ramsey, was to preach, and at a diocesan garden party afterwards. Her Royal Highness went first to Nottingham, and after a formal reception by the Lord Mayor, she spent two hours on a local housing estate and had lunch informally in one of the council houses, getting to Southwell just in time for the service. We gave a lunch party for the notables in the Great Hall of the Manor — Wolsey's banqueting hall during his last phase. The Provost had made immense preparations and the service in the minster was magnificent. The Princess must have been thoroughly tired, but she stayed an hour or two at the garden party, moving about among the guests on a horrid drizzly afternoon and giving the greatest pleasure to everybody. But my own recollections of all this are not nearly so clear as might be expected. I was in great pain during the whole proceedings, but managed to stick it out and play my part until Princess Margaret had left. An hour later my doctor was driving me to hospital to undergo a severe operation, which put me out of action for three months. (She sent me a charming letter when she read about it.) But I am anticipating the sequence.

In December 1954 Lilian and I kept our silver wedding. We threw two parties, at Southwell and in London, and were deeply moved at the gathering in the Manor when the mayors of the Nottinghamshire boroughs presented us with some silver entrée dishes. Just about that time some post-war credits came in and, for once, we decided that we would 'blue' the money. Bishop Craske offered me a temporary chaplaincy, to take the Christmas services at Taormina. So off we went, with Rosemary to Sicily, showing her Rome for two or three days en route, and had a vastly enjoyable Christmas holiday. We were only away for two or three weeks but the silver wedding seemed to deserve that much.

Some time before this we acquired a home of our own. Forty years and more before, as an undergraduate, I had started going to Seatoller House, or some other farmhouse, in Borrowdale, to do sustained reading during the long vacation, and of course long walks on the fells. (That was before there were any motor cars, and one drove out from Keswick on a coach and four and the farms used to charge 35s. a week.) I have been there almost every year since. Borrowdale became my Innisfree. After our marriage I took Lilian there and with her too it was love at first sight. Hardly one year have we missed a Cumberland holiday. For years on end we stayed at Manesty Farm. But not long after the Lambeth Conference there came onto the market a small house, standing on Catbells above Derwentwater and with a superb view over the Scafell range; and one look was enough to decide. Harry Baines, then Rector of Rugby, and I scraped up whatever we had and bought it, sharing the house together. For years the Barrys and the Baineses had joint holidays. When he was elected Bishop of Wellington, New Zealand, it was clearly no more use to them and we took over their share in the ownership. This little house, The Coppice at Manesty, has brought endless happiness to our family; and still now during school holidays it is a home for three generations.

I had been at Cyril Garbett's eightieth birthday party, not

long before that pilgrimage to the Holy Land from which he came back to York to die. The party, held in Admiralty House, was arranged for him by his former chaplains. (I had been an examining chaplain years before and was allowed to scrape in on that ticket.) But one remarkable thing about the party was that almost everyone there was a bishop. His chaplains were by way of becoming bishops!

After his operation and long illness he died at the end of 1955 before his resignation had taken effect. He had finished his course, but I missed him grievously. He had been a close and staunch friend to both of us and a wonderful godfather to Rosemary. Almost to the last his vigour was unabated. Yet probably he held on too long. On the other hand, I think it is most unlikely that he would have written his big books, as Gore wrote his *Trilogy*, after retirement. Cyril drew his strength and confidence from his office, and stripped of it he would have been a shorn Samson.

Who would be his successor in the Archbishopric? George Bell might even now have come for five years and had, it seems, been led to understand that he was to be offered the nomination, which he was prepared to accept. Failing George, there was nobody in the South, and Ramsey was the ablest man among us. During the short time that he was at York he showed me much kindness and consideration. I had hoped to see Leslie Hunter go to Durham. Yet when Maurice Harland, an old friend of mine, came I was happy to have him as a colleague.

I have already told how in my younger days I had many contacts with Fr. Herbert Kelly. When I became Bishop of Southwell I found myself Visitor of Kelham — a prospect by which, at first, I was slightly alarmed, for I knew very little about religious communities. But it very soon came to mean a great deal to me. Some of its members had been with me at Knutsford. Herbert Kelly was now becoming senile, but I knew three successive Directors intimately, Reginald Tribe (who was killed in an air raid in London), Stephen Bedale (two years senior to me at Oxford) and, in the later years of my time, Paul Hume; and I was in the House as often as could be managed. And the House gave me one of my best friendships.

The parish of Averham was a family living with a long succession of patrician rectors. After the death of the last incumbent — a superb parish priest of the older squarson type — the Community acquired the patronage, and their first appointment was Stephen Bedale. The idea was to give him a rest; but he could not be happy outside the walls of the House and went back to it after only a few years. They then appointed Fr. Nicholas Allenby, who soon became active and prominent in the diocese and worked with me on a number of different projects. It was he, for example, who undertook the laborious job of editing and producing the *Southwell Review* in its first critical stages. And shamelessly I asked more and more of him. I was at this time without a personal chaplain. (Eric Lunn, who had served me devotedly after Noel Turner, was soon to move off to Yattendon.) It was one of the wisest things I have done when I persuaded him to take on the job. Nicholas became an intimate friend of the family, and I cannot tell how much I owe to his help. After some years the Community directed him to take charge of the daughter house in South Australia. But when he came home after that tour of duty the Archbishop of Canterbury appointed him to the missionary Bishopric of Kuching (Sarawak) and there fell to me the joyful privilege of presenting him for consecration.

A small diocese can attract first-class men, but it has not enough first-class posts to retain them. A remarkable number of clergy from Southwell have moved on to wider responsibilities. At the 1968 Lambeth Conference, in which, of course, I had no part or lot, I was invited to dine with a group of Bishops who had previously worked with me in the diocese. There were seven hosts and there were several others (two already retired) who could not make it.[8] Recent appointments would

[8] The hosts were Chichester, Portsmouth, Carlisle, Kuching, Worcester, Taunton, Stockport. 'Possibles' included Wakefield (Ramsbotham, retired),

add three more to the total. I hope that evening gave my hosts as much pleasure as it gave me.

During the fifties I was reinforced by the advent of another assistant bishop. Many years before I had gone with some men from Knutsford, led by James Welch, afterwards so well-known as religious Director at the BBC, to give a hand with a boys' holiday camp run by the parish of St. Gabriel, Sunderland, where Jimmy had started life as a choirboy. The vicar of the parish was called Lasbrey, afterwards Bishop of Nigeria, and he had a new deacon called Morris Gelsthorpe, a tough rugger player, who, during the first war, had served as a private soldier, a captain of machine-gunners, and as a pilot. I had been in touch with him, on and off, ever since; and every reader of missionary literature knew about his episcopate in Africa, first as Suffragan in Nigeria, afterwards in the Sudan, where he had become Bishop Gwynne's successor.

When I heard that he was about to retire, I asked Anthony Bevir at No. 10 to keep the Crown living of Bingham vacant, and was overjoyed when Morris agreed to accept it. For him it was in some ways a homecoming, for his family came from the Nottingham-Derbyshire border, and he was constantly finding the Gelsthorpe name in Bingham churchyard and in other neighbouring villages.

He and his Elfrida (they were recently married) brought invaluable help to me and made themselves felt throughout the whole life of the diocese, where he was universally loved and trusted — and not least by the Anglo-Catholic clergy. (As he had a lifelong CMS background, this is some measure of his breadth of sympathy.) During my illness and when I was abroad he shouldered the whole burden of the diocese. During part of the time, his old chief, Bishop Lasbrey, came to live with them in Bingham rectory. And every year, almost till his death, Gwynne

Grantham (Anthony Otter, retired), Penrith (Victor Turner, retired, now deceased). To these there can since be added Kenneth Thompson of Sherwood, Foskett of Penrith and Hare Duke of St. Andrews. Richard Hanson, Professor at Nottingham, has been elected Bishop of Clogher.

came there on an annual visit, so that I was able to keep touch up to the end. Morris confided to me that his years at Southwell had been the happiest in his whole ministry. Certainly we were exceedingly happy to have him — a saintly man and a great Christian bishop. I hope there may soon be a worthy biography of him.

Lord Fisher once told me that every diocesan Bishop must expect to be doing at least two whole-time jobs; and for five or six years at least that was true for me. As I mentioned above (p. 158) the work of the post-war Church was weakened and in some places crippled by lack of ministerial manpower. This was so particularly in the North. People who lived in places like Oxford or the seaside resorts of the South never could be got to believe the story. It was not merely an *ad hoc* post-war problem. The Bishops had talked about it for half a century. And year by year the *Crockford* editorials had been calling the attention of the Church to the steady decline in the number of ordinations, and trying to make its flesh creep with warnings: a curate will soon be as rare as a dodo. There was not, and so far as I know never has been, any reliable calculation to show exactly how many clergy the Church needed — or even how many it could afford to pay. Shortage was therefore a rather ambiguous word: of what standard were we falling short? It was perfectly clear that the number of men ordained had been getting gradually smaller than it was in the mid-nineteenth century; and a series of tables had been produced to show the number of ordinations annually which were needed to get back to the pre-war total. (But arguably there had been too many then, as there certainly had been in the eighteenth century and after the Napoleonic Wars, when there was a large influx of ex-officers and not enough employment to go round.) But there was now a much bigger population. And, without defining an optimum ratio, it is surely evident that if the ratio of clergy to population is constantly falling there is bound to be a decline in Church membership — as is happening before our eyes today. And the post-war situation was very dangerous. In the North, at least, there were many parishes with populations of 10,000 or more which were being worked by single-handed incumbents, some of whom were rapidly breaking down (I had perhaps twenty of these in my own diocese.) Moreover, when ordinands are in a seller's market and are fully alive to that situation — so that a candidate interviews the bishop, rather than the bishop a candidate — Bournemouth is going to get more than Birmingham. There was real danger that it would be impossible even to keep the parochial system going, to say nothing of any hope of a forward movement. Urgently, we must have more men. It was no good now trying to overtake the accumulated deficit of the war years. But the new intake must somehow be increased to, say, 600 or 700 annually if the Church was to carry on at all. The average age of the clergy in England at this time was sixty, if not higher, and the new intake did not equal the natural wastage, so the shortage would soon become even more acute.

In an attempt to meet this situation the Bishops agreed, advised by CACTM, to set up a powerful recruitment committee, and the Archbishops asked me to be chairman of it. This seemed to be just up my street, and with Michael Brown as secretary at CACTM, I threw myself into the new job with enthusiasm. And at first it did take nearly the whole of my time. It was not a question of going around pathetically pleading with men to offer themselves for Orders to save a weakening Church from collapse. The supply from the public schools had fallen lamentably. But nothing, probably, can be more useless than for a bishop to go and preach at a school, or university, and appeal for men. It tends to provoke boredom or ribaldry. (At St. Mary's, I used to beg bishops not to mention it.) The problem has to be dealt with far more radically. A fighting army does not 'appeal', it *drafts* men. The Church must not sit waiting for volunteers — the twelve apostles were not volunteers — it must go out and look for the men it needs, and claim them.

Bishop Walter Frere said more than once that it had been a disastrous mistake when the Church had come to lay almost exclusive emphasis on the interior 'call' to Holy Orders. (It is a familiar fact that the weakest candidates, and by any rational standard the least fitted, are often invincibly certain of having been 'called'.) The call should come initially from the Church — meaning the Church, not merely its officials — and it had now to be publicly proclaimed. No committee, meeting in Westminster, could hope to supply the Church with the men it needed. All it could do was to get the facts presented and to try to stimulate local effort, in the dioceses and the parishes. If anything was to happen at all, the whole Church had got to be in on this.

The word 'recruitment' came under criticism, as suggesting a kind of psychological press-gang. That was not in the least what we intended by it. What we meant was a resolute effort to secure that all concerned did hear the call, and hear it as something that might be addressed to themselves. Then as now, young men were saying that the Ministry was a marginal activity. Men who would in the past have been ordained were now opting for other forms of Christian ministry, leaving ordination out of account as something that nobody would consider seriously, however strong his commitment to Christian service. It was that trend that had to be reversed. The Ministry had to be got back on to the map again, and presented as something which could claim, and needed, the strongest and ablest men available, not the leavings of other professions. What was wanted now, on the widest possible scale, was a church-wide publicity campaign to put the claim of the Ministry across, in the schools and universities, in industry, in the forces (national service was still on), in the professions, everywhere where men were, and letting them know what it was and what it involved, and what kinds of qualities it could use.

It was this that our committee sought to initiate; and I drove my fellow Bishops nearly mad by speaking about it at every Bishops' meeting, putting the subject down every time, so that it should be permanently on the agenda. Of course it entailed a great deal of work, in committee meetings, in local conferences, in visits to schools and universities, in approaches to local education authorities and professional bodies, in running exhibitions and so forth, and in constant travelling around the dioceses. Among the happiest of these activities were the annual school-boy conferences at Oxford, which were nearly always over-subscribed and were later extended to other centres as well. At these no pressure whatever was applied, and we never allowed the heat to be turned on. We told them frankly and fully about the Ministry in its various forms and opportunities, in its disappointments and its rewards, and answered any questions they wanted to ask. Then they had the data for making their own decisions, which was the avowed object of the conference. Many eminent men came to speak for us at these weeks, even, once, the Archbishop of Canterbury, and they were inspiring occasions. At one of them, I remember, a bright boy, opening conversation with me at dinner, asked, "Have you ever been in Oxford before, sir?" As I said at the time, *sic transit gloria mundi*.

Our efforts were in no sense a failure. The curve began to go up and rose to a peak, though since then it has again fallen alarmingly, and we staved off disaster at least for the time being. But I never ceased insisting to my colleagues that the prime consideration was quality. If any profession seems to be in low water, put up the requirements — the Army learnt that long ago. When recruitment was flagging in the first war, the War Office raised the chest measurement. The more you ask for, the more you will get. If the Church gives the impression that it is prepared to accept men who could not make a living elsewhere, the more gifted will certainly look in another direction. To lower the standard in order to fill up the ranks is, for the Church, a policy of suicide. But for this I found it hard to win more than lip-service. I fear that the Church has, on the whole, been too ready to think more of quantity than quality. I still believe that if we had been brave enough to require higher standards of qualification, we should have got more men as well as better men. And in the situation in which we now are, a sub-standard Ministry may do positive harm.

My committee's report, *Supply of fit persons*, I introduced myself to the Assembly, in the only major speech I ever inflicted on it. Then and there it served quite a useful purpose. Some of my own reflections on the whole subject went into a short book, *Vocation and Ministry*, which was published just in time for the Lambeth Conference.

At the Lambeth Conference 1958 I renewed old friendships and made many new ones. Before it began, we had a group of bishops from overseas staying in the Manor for their peregrination of the diocese in the 'Lambeth Walk' which precedes the conference. And at weekends, during the conference itself, we would drive two or three to Southwell, getting them back to London on Sunday night. This time Lilian stayed with me in London so that we were able to share together in some of the many and varied social functions laid on by the hospitality committee; and all of these of course brought new contacts with men from all over the world, and perhaps their wives. One of the best results of these conferences is that bishops of the Anglican communion the world over know one another personally.

The previous conference may have been more exciting, because for most of us it was our first experience. But this one did better thinking, and in many ways 1958 was a big advance on 1948. What attracted most public notice was the very important report on the Family, which had been prepared (for once) with expert briefing. By its emphasis on family planning and its consequential acceptance of contraceptives — which had been uncompromisingly condemned by the conference of 1930 and shyly glanced at in 1948 — it reversed a traditional Christian ethical judgement which had been unquestioned all down the centuries and was held to be rooted in 'natural law'. This was courageous and realistic leadership. (Many years before when, in a tract on marriage, I had made some mild suggestions in this direction, the book was banned by the Mothers' Union, while Lindsay and his wife told me roundly that it was a betrayal of Christian moral standards.) The debate was powerfully led by Stephen Bayne, who was one of the dominant figures at the conference, and made so deep an impression on the bishops that he was not left to enjoy his Olympia. Almost inevitably he was chosen to be the first holder of the new post of Anglican executive officer.

I made a few short speeches at Lambeth but did not take any prominent part this time. Younger men were coming along by now. I did make a vain attempt to defeat an 'appeal for peace' in the name of the bishops. This kind of thing seems to me to be rather bleating. What the bishops ought to have shouted for was Justice. Otherwise I did not speak more than a few times. But though I contributed little of any importance, very important events for us resulted from this conference. One of the main subjects that year was the structures and training of the Ministry. On this I was thought to be some kind of authority, and quite a number of overseas Bishops invited me to pay them a visit and help with these questions in their dioceses. When there is a legitimate chance of going places I do not need to be asked more than once, if it is at all possible to accept. In the next few months other invitations came in, from the General Synod of the Canadian Church, from Melbourne, from Johannesburg and elsewhere. Clearly not all of these would be practicable, but most of them now began to fit into a pattern which would mean a tour right round the world. I was eager to go. But how could we find the money? And could another long absence be justified? My Archbishop blessed it and urged me to go. Archbishop Fisher kindly made me a grant from a fund under his control at Lambeth, and a wealthy layman in the diocese gave me a very substantial cheque. So it seemed to be on; I got the plans worked out, and in February 1959 we set out again on our travels, bound, for the second time, for Australia. (Rosemary was by this time married.)

We went direct, by sea, the whole way from Tilbury. This trip gave us a day at Gibraltar — a Sunday. We went to the sung

Eucharist in the cathedral and the Dean had arranged for us to be shown the sights.

The Bishops of the Anglican communion are a very closely organised trade union — this is perhaps still more the case with their wives — so that if you are travelling with your card you can count on it that at every port the local bishop, or his representative, will come aboard and carry you off for the day. You are thus able to see and to learn far more, even in a very limited time, than would be possible for a private tourist. At Aden the Anglican chaplain took charge of us, and we spent the day at Colombo with the Bishop. In the evening we were entertained at dinner in magnificent local style by Archdeacon de Sousa (now Bishop of Colombo) whom I had known as an Oxford undergraduate.

Sailing in tropical waters always fascinates me, but it had been rather a long voyage and we were glad when we arrived at Fremantle. Lilian had some GFS functions there, after which she rejoined the ship and went round to Melbourne, while I spent a long weekend at Perth, occupied mainly in the university (which has one of the finest campuses in the world) and then flew overnight to Melbourne, on which we were to be based for the next few weeks as the guests of Archbishop Frank Woods. In Melbourne there was a pretty full programme — preachments in the cathedral and other churches, a long clergy school (the real point of my coming) and much talking to students of various kinds.

The Archbishop and others were deeply concerned about the training of the Australian Ministry, which was, indeed, one of their most urgent problems if the Church was to lead the new Australia. The poorly trained and half-educated clergy with which it had to make do in the early days simply could not meet the changed situation and could even bring the Church into contempt. In the course of many conversations I began to see that the root cause of the weakness was the breach between the Church and the universities, from all of which theology was excluded. (I believe that this is no longer entirely the case.)

What the Church of England had done by choice — and, as we can see now, a gravely mistaken choice — in Australia it had done by necessity. It had to teach men in its own theological colleges, some with very poor academic standards, in isolation from university life, and had tried to run its own school of theology, conferring diplomas and even doctorates which had no recognised academic standing. It seemed to me, therefore, that nothing could do more for the future strength of the Church in Victoria than a strong theological faculty at Melbourne. That was, at the time, being tentatively considered, and at the official university sermon I argued for it as strongly as I could, from the point of view of the university, not merely because of the help it would give the Church.

From Melbourne we were sent out on short visits to a number of other places and other States. We had a delicious weekend in Tasmania, with a preachment in Hobart cathedral, and afterwards spent some days in South Australia. My chief objective there was St. Michael's House, the Kelham centre for training ordinands, of which Allenby was now prior. It is high up in the ranges above Adelaide. I gave some talks and had many conversations, and had a great and even uproarious time there, for all the rules were off for my visit; they even gave a lunch-party for Lilian. I also talked to the sixth form at St. Peter's school, Adelaide, and spent a long day with the Bishop in his cottage. We had, also, again, a few days at Canberra, housed in the graduate school of the university.

Subsequently we were moved on to Sydney, where the Dean gave us charming hospitality, and there was the usual round of sermons and lectures, with one long excursion into the ranges, and dinner one evening with a Barry cousin, now President of the Australian Medical Association. Thence to Brisbane, the furthest north we reached. At Brisbane, the aged Archbishop Halse, who had in his youth been a student at Kelham, asked me to speak in his theological college. I gave them what I thought were some original and, as I hoped, provocative ideas about the Christian faith and their future ministry; and afterwards told the chairman that I was sorry if I had upset his young men too much. "It didn't upset me," said the old Archbishop. "I felt quite at home with what you said. It was what Fr. Kelly told us when we were boys."

Thence we flew back to Sydney and sailed for Auckland. I should like to think that I did anything useful to repay the Church in Australia for its kindness to us. I had learnt very much that I did not know before. But what now remains with me most vividly is my delight in the South Pacific area, its skies by night, its flowers and its sunshine. "Thou deckest thyself with light as it were with a garment." If I had nobody but myself to think about, that is where I should go to end my days.

New Zealand was entirely unknown to us, and the programme included only about three weeks. Archdeacon Beere, who had been a student at Knutsford, collected us from the ship at Auckland and almost before we had found our legs I was involved in discussions about clergy training with some of the staff of St. John's theological college, founded by the great Bishop Selwyn. (A few years later I made my contribution by advising the Church to appoint Raymond Foster, one of my first ordinands, as Principal.) After lunch there arrived John Holland, Bishop of Waikato (now of Polynesia) who drove us off to his see-town of Hamilton. There were many meetings and utterances arranged for me. But we had the immensely interesting experience of seeing something of the Maori villages and were shown the geysers of the Waikato country. And a former Southwell incumbent, Kinross Nicholson, had us to stay and took us to the mysterious — I had almost written, mystic — glow-worm cavern. In the South Island we had a week at Christchurch (where I first met the present Dean of St. Paul's) as guests of the Bishop, Alwyn Warren, with a number of sermons, meetings and discussions about the way ordinands were trained, or weren't, and a memorable day in the Southern Alps. There were a few days with the Archbishop at Wellington, which I had so long wanted to see with my own eyes because my godfather had years ago been bishop there, and saw the great new cathedral going up to replace the lovely original wooden church. Thence by bus the whole way back to Auckland where we spent the final days at Bishopscourt, and I gave my last sermon, in the cathedral. We had fallen in love with New Zealand and were sad that the time to leave came so soon. At Auckland we embarked for Vancouver.

The ship put in for a day at Suva, where Bishop Kempthorne showed us as much as was possible, and the diocese gave us a multiracial lunch-party. I learnt with surprise that in the cathedral they had to have Holy Communion in Hindi — so ubiquitous is the Indian trader. I spent some hours with the bishop in discussion of the future of his theological college, which then consisted of two men from the islands. I was fired with imagining its possibilities as eventually a constituent element in the university of the South Pacific (there was already a medical school in Fiji) and urged him to work towards that end. On my return to Southwell, the diocese sent him a gift of nearly £1,000 by way of starting an endowment fund for it. I am happy to think that we had some little share in the birth of the present Pacific School of Divinity. The only other call on the long voyage across the vast Pacific was at Hawaii, where Bishop and Mrs. Kennedy showed us everything — as exciting a day as we have ever spent — and I met the diocesan clergy in the evening.

At Vancouver Godfrey Gower was waiting for us, with a full programme of preachings and meetings. A layman, hitherto quite unknown to me, had us to stay as his guests in Vancouver Island; then we started once more on the transcontinental journey. I had an official date in Toronto, where I met the committee of the General Synod, by whom we were sumptuously entertained, and explained to them the workings of CACTM; thence for the final night in Montreal, which we spent with the Dean and Dr. Eric Jay.

I had spent the voyage out in preparing lectures. On the voyage back I had written them up in book form and they were published as *Asking the Right Questions*.

This had been a quite wonderful experience. I can only hope that we gave as much as we got, and that something at least of what had been given to me was now in some way passed on to my own diocese. There followed two years of intensive work at Southwell. I was now, I think, at the height of my powers mentally, and physically things were a good bit easier since the Commissioners had taken me over and given me a chauffeur and more secretarial help in the person of Group Captain Butler. But I was now within six months of seventy, and could not expect to go on forever. Yet before I faced the question of retirement, there was one climactic experience in store. In my younger days I had caught from J. H. Oldham a deep concern about African education, and of course like any good little Anglican I was brought up on the romance of the UMCA. Zanzibar and Victoria Nyanza had been magic names to me from my boyhood, and I passionately wanted to see East Africa. Two years later the opportunity came, through an invitation from Archbishop Leonard Beecher, and just before Christmas 1961 we sailed from Genoa to Mombasa.

In many ways this was to mean more to me than all the other journeys added together. This was the first time I had been in contact with first-generation Christian converts, and that — though it came to me so late in life — cannot but be a decisive experience. I did a good deal of lecturing in Nairobi, preached at an ordination in Mombasa and now at last not only saw the cathedral in Zanzibar but preached in it, by interpreter. The Archbishop gave us opportunity to visit a number of centres in Kenya, including some stations way out in the bush, and I spoke in some of the most important of the grammar schools for boys and for girls. The people, the country, the sense of a dream come true, all made this a quite unforgettable month, for which we can never be grateful enough to the Beechers.

After this followed a fortnight in Uganda, first in the north with Bishop Usher Wilson, who gave me quite a lot of speaking to do, and showed us everything within reach. Thence, after a long enchanting drive past the sources of the Nile at Jinja (I cannot convey the excitement this gave me) we went for a week or so to Makerere, which had long been for me a dream-place, through Oldham, Alec Fraser and Robert Stopford. The vice-chancellor, Sir Bernard de Bunsen, whom I had known well since his boyhood (his parents lived in my parish in West-minster), introduced us to everything and everybody. It was a deep satisfaction to preach in the college chapel on Sunday evening, when I handed over to them a gift from the students at Nottingham university.

We went on to stay with Archbishop Leslie Brown at Kam-pala, where we were entertained in the house that had been built by Bishop Willis, who had first awakened my interest in Uganda. But all this time our whole tour had been overclouded by extremely disquieting news about our family; and this had by now become so alarming that we felt obliged to cut out the rest of the programme and fly home at once from Entebbe. (We arrived in London in a snowstorm.)

I did my best to pass on to the diocese what had been given to me in East Africa. For, simple and commonplace though it may sound today, when East Africa is included in package holidays, that trip had done something to me in my depths. But only a few weeks after our return home, our family was overwhelmed in a tragedy which had a dreadful publicity at the time, but about which I still cannot trust myself to speak. The diocese stood by us magnificently, and, as so often happens in a parson's life, the grief brought me closer to my people and enriched my pastoral relations with them. They saw me not as a high priest on a *cathedra* but as a vulnerable and stricken man, needing their ministry and support. And when I now tell people in deep distress that "Nothing can separate us from the love of God", I am not merely quoting a pious text; I am telling them something that I have known to be true.

But I was now in my seventy-third year and the time was near when I must withdraw from office. I had sometimes advised senior clergy, "Make your decision while you are free to make it and while you can still walk out on your own feet.

Don't wait till you lose control of the situation, and have to be wheeled out in a chair — or carried out on the shoulders of four other men." This must now have a personal application. There were voices that urged, 'Stay just one more year'. But I knew that then it would be 'Just one more', till at last I became incapable of believing that the Church of England could exist without me. So after working on for a few more months, I sought Her Majesty's leave to resign the See. I did not at all want to leave the diocese, and I should have been happy to work for a little longer with, or under, Archbishop Donald Coggan.

I had done what I could to stand for the Great Church, not solely for the C. of E., and had therefore attempted to do whatever was possible to foster relations with other Christian communions. I had inherited from my predecessor an organisation called the Christian Front, which bravely staged a number of public meetings, in which all the Churches took part, for Christian moral witness during the war years. But they never seemed to me to get very far — not least because of the Roman Catholic ruling that no kind of common prayer was allowed.[9] Though the Roman Catholic Bishop of Nottingham and I were friends, little headway was made in that direction; how changed is the situation since then! But, as John Rawlinson said in one of his books, reunion must start where it can; and between the Anglican diocese and the Free Churches there were the closest possible relations. Ministers sometimes referred to me as 'our bishop'. Towards the end of my time we had been able to achieve a good measure of co-operation in a strongly Methodist centre like Nottingham. We had, for example, reached agreement to build only one church in new districts instead of a number of competing conventicles, and were beginning to learn to worship together. All this may sound little enough now; I claim no more than that we did our best in the situation in which we then were. The tides of the Spirit have carried us far

[9] On this at Nottingham, see the extract from Garbett's diary in Smyth's *Life*, p. 362.

since that time. But I found it personally very touching when, during my last summer in the diocese, the Free Churches invited me to a farewell garden party.

The summer closed with the Toronto conference. A generous private gift at the last moment made it possible for Lilian to come with me, and we were the guests of Bishop Wilkinson. As a reunion of friends from all over the world — and I could not but know that in all probability I was seeing some of them for the last time — it was an immensely enjoyable finale. And Canadian hospitality is fabulous. A very good time indeed was had by all. But as a conference, it was disappointing; and there were some very disturbing undercurrents, about which I shall have a word to say in the next chapter.

Maddeningly enough, when we returned home I had a rather serious accident, which kept me immobilised till the autumn. So there could be none of the usual leave takings and I could not even say farewell to the clergy. I could only hobble in to a gathering which had been arranged in the Minster, when the Provost handed me a cheque generously subscribed by the parishes.

I ceased to be Bishop of Southwell on St. Luke's day, 1963, twenty-two years after my consecration.

IX

Autumn Fruit

WHEN I WAS appointed to Southwell there were friends who
thought it would be an anticlimax, rather than, as a diocese is
to most men, the climax of my ministerial life. And I may have
been better known as a Canon of Westminster, operating under
my own name, than I was disguised behind an official signature
— which I used for so long that I still inadvertently write it, in
letters and even on my cheques. Certainly I had never expected
to spend nearly half my working ministry as a bishop in the
industrial east Midlands; but that was the work which was
given me to do. Perhaps if it had not been for my disability
Southwell might not have been the last stop. But in retrospect I
do not in the least regret those twenty-two years in Nottinghamshire. If I had stayed on at Westminster indefinitely I
should very likely have grown stale and lazy, and my colleagues
would certainly have had too much of me till they levered me
into some minor deanery, to sink into comfortable ineffective-
ness. But, though in weaker moments I may have hankered for
the mellow dignities of a southern close, I shall always be glad
to have worked for so long in the North, where the Church is at
once most hard-pressed and most vigorous. I should be surprised if, in the Province of York, they are writing God's
obituary notices. Since the war began we had hardly been south
of the Thames. Returning now to London and the home
counties we seem to have moved back into a different world,
and, in all sorts of ways, a different Church, which, though it
has more resources and amenities, I would not be prepared to
describe as a stronger Church.

For now we have come right back again on our tracks. Years

before, when we bought the little house at Manesty, we had thought of it as a home for retirement. When it came to the point, however, we realised that the middle of space was no location as a permanent home for two elderly people. As Herbert Williams said, when he retired to Chester, "When you have one foot in the grave you need to have the other on a bus stop!" At Manesty we should have been five miles from a shop and four hundred from our family in Sussex, and in winter we could have been entirely cut off. So, after exploring other possibilities and elaborate financial calculations, we decided to try to come back to Westminster, and were lucky enough to secure a tiny flat in St. John's parish and almost touching the church. I could hardly be nearer to my past than that. It is a happiness to see St. John's splendidly restored by its Friends and again in use as a centre of music and worship — 'secularised' but serving Christian ends.

We are very glad to have made that decision. At Westminster there is so much laid on, and you are almost sure to meet someone sometimes. We had a few old friends from the parish still here, and I value the contacts with the Abbey, where I am accorded a kind of Old Boy status. Moreover, my vicar and long-term successor, Bill Davidson, is one of my own 'sons' who had been ordained at Southwell many years ago. So, here is our new home and we are well content.

I was supposed now to be past work and about to 'enjoy that well-earned leisure' about which so many speeches have been made. I had vaguely thought of retirement as a time when one could at last cultivate a rock-garden and re-read Homer and Virgil and the Greek plays. But it seems that in fact it is not till he retires that a man knows what really hard work can be. I seem to have far less leisure now than I used to have, which is, on balance, something to be thankful for. The alternative might be vacuity and boredom and fatty degeneration of the faculties.

The first few months I did find very hard to bear. One seemed to be totally useless and unwanted, with no job to do and no function to discharge. Once out, as Garbett used to say, you *are* out. Before long, however, I began to realise that if you try to get back to a world which is closed to you, it will merely break your heart and destroy your soul. What we had to do was to summon up our courage to make a new start and begin all over again, building up for ourselves a new little world and finding, if possible, new forms of ministry. Incidentally, too, I must try to earn some money, for pensioners living on a fixed income, and one that was fixed more than ten years ago, are in a very difficult position.

That winter we spent some of the gift from Southwell on a wonderful holiday at Bordighera, where we had a fortnight of unbroken sunshine, and came back ready to make ourselves a future.

By the kindly good offices of the Bishop of London I had been elected some months before this to one of the ancient endowed city lectureships known as the St. Antholin's lecture. The lectures under this trust were to start in January, and it had been arranged with the rector that they should be in St. Michael's, Cornhill. And nothing better than that could have happened, for it gave me a spiritual home. I tried to do what I always had been doing, that is, to offer an interpretation of the fundamental Christian beliefs for the seeker and the still un-committed — though in the event those who came to listen were from the inner circle of the faithful. The trustees renewed the appointment for two years more. For the second course I tried to expound some of the elements of Christian ethics, on which, for other reasons, I was then working; and the third was a popular study of the Gospels, which I hoped might not be regarded as too highbrow. I am bound to admit that the response was pitiful, and this was a new experience for me, so long accustomed to crowded congregations. What attracts popular attention nowadays is not what is said but 'names' and notorieties; who would go to listen to a retired bishop? But as I was told that one of my predecessors had spoken throughout to an audience of one I may have been more fortunate than some others.

The lectures may have been largely barren effort. But to me, in my personal life, the giving of them brought a reward out of all proportion. For week by week during those three years I was brought into close contact with the rector and enjoyed long and intimate conversation with him. This ripened into a friendship with Norman Motley which has helped me more than I can say here. And when I ceased to give lectures he invited me to stay on as a part-time member of his staff. This gave me exactly what I most needed — a church, a centre of rich pastoral ministry, to which I belonged and in which I could feel at home, and could, from time to time, celebrate and preach. And, as I was to learn, one of the churchwardens had been at Balliol while I was chaplain there.

But further than that, in preparing for the lectures I had done a considerable amount of reading and collected a good deal of new material; and I did not see why this need be wasted. So I worked up the notes for the first course into a short book, which David Edwards encouraged me to publish as a paperback called *Questioning Faith*, the title being intended to suggest both the presentation of positive belief and the open, sceptical mind which still asks questions. That little book has done surprisingly well, both in this country and in the USA, and seems to have been what a good many people wanted. But it was only one more 'little book', and I now felt the urge to try something more ambitious.

In November 1964 I delivered the Gore lecture in the Abbey, on Christian faith and secular society. The reflection and reading involved in the preparation of it opened for me a new world of thought on the real meaning of 'secularisation' and the place of the Church and the ethics of Christianity in the pluralist, post-Christendom society. I wanted now to explore this more deeply, and I spent the next few months in extensive reading (which supplied material for the lunchtime lectures) and making the first drafts of a larger book. What emerged from all this was, what I hoped might be something more like a major work, *Christian Ethics and Secular Society*, to which I have referred in an earlier chapter. It received exceptionally good reviews and brought me something approaching a fan-mail. So I felt that I could not be quite senile yet. One limitation, as I can see now, is that it did not sufficiently relate ethical enquiry as such to the solvents of analytic philosophy, or give the student material enough for belief in the objectivity of values. I could make a rather better book of it now. But, so far as it went, I feel no need to apologise for it. It is being used pretty widely in the colleges, and is still, I am informed, selling quietly.

There remained the talks I had given on the Gospels. After laborious and intensive study of some of the critical questions involved (which lies behind the text but is not mentioned in it) I wrote these up into a popular book — perhaps deceptively simple on the surface, for there is much more in it than meets the eye — which the publishers called *Weep Not For Me*. That, too, had an encouraging reception and is being used in some schools and colleges. So three books came out of those elementary lectures, and in old age I had again 'commenced author'.

Meanwhile, I was taking on other pieces of work. Trevor Beeson, who hails from Southwell diocese, asked me to review theological books for *New Christian*, and every few weeks I do a piece for them. Occasionally, too, I review a book for *Frontier* or for *Theology* or for *The Times Literary Supplement*. Lately, I have been again asked to do some Saturday articles for *The Times* — for which, in fact, I was writing anonymously nearly all the time I was at Southwell. And during the last three years, to my great surprise, I have been asked to do some part-time teaching at the Berkshire College of Education, where I take Religious Education students in their final year in Ethics and the Philosophy of Religion. I learnt as a bishop how important the teachers in schools are to the Christian cause and how much support they need from the Church. I have welcomed the chance of trying to help them — across the gulf of two generations.

Preaching is something I now find rather laborious. One quickly loses that dreadful facility which one is compelled to acquire while in office. But how welcome a change is the absence of reporters. In his public utterances a bishop is thinking all the time, with part of his mind, Whatever will this look like to-morrow morning? Now I can talk quietly and directly to the congregation actually in front of me. And though what I say now may be less exciting, I should like to believe that it is better stuff. But everything now takes much longer than it used to take. Old men work slowly, and tire quickly, so that all these various activities seem to leave no time for that 'leisure'. But together they add up to a teaching ministry, which is now the one contribution open to me.

I mention here that in 1966 Lilian's work for the GFS was recognised, when her name was submitted by the Prime Minister for an OBE in the birthday honours, which gave both of us great satisfaction. By a strange coincidence, my brother Harold appeared in the same list with a CBE, and they went to Buckingham Palace together. She still works for the GFS in the London diocese. So she, too, has now many activities on her own account. Thus, between the two of us we have succeeded in building round us a new little world of our own, with new interests, new contacts and new friends, and have been blessed with the physical health to do it. And so far, by meticulous budgeting, we have managed an annual fortnight with the Swiss flowers, and our year is planned round that as its chief event. There is very much to be thankful for.

But "Scribble, scribble, scribble, Mr. Gibbon" — I have never been able to stop scribbling. Apart from some crude, forgotten juvenilia — of which I should now hate to be reminded — I must have perpetrated at least fifteen books, five of which have been written since my retirement. Three of these I have mentioned already. But since then, on top of my various other activities, I have added two more to the total. Just before Dr. Dillistone's great work[1] appeared — and the timing was fortunate for me, otherwise mine would have been overshadowed — I

[1] *The Christian Understanding of Atonement* (Nisbet, 1968).

rashly published a study of *The Atonement*, a subject on which I had long been pondering, and tried to suggest some new lines of approach. This has been published also in America.

But that book, though I hope it may fairly be called 'liberal', was within the mainstream tradition. And in order to review 'new' theology, I have had to make some attempt to understand it and the philosophy which lies behind it; all this time, therefore, I have been still learning. In the bleak thought-world of the 'radical' theologians, almost lunar in its lack of atmosphere, what has evaporated or been obscured, is the transcendent *mysterium tremendum*. (The same seems to me to be also true about some of the new liturgical forms now offered to us.) And in this it reflects our positivistic age. Most 'modernisms' are reductionist. Indeed, there is a kind of perennial modernism, sometimes dignified as Higher Thought, at all times mostly the same and mostly nonsense, which has tried to enter the Church from the beginning. I have travelled a long theological journey through many ports of call named 'new theology', but I had not expected to find Christians doubtful about the reality of God, or recommending acceptance of Christian atheism. Secular or radical theologians are attempting, wholly rightly and legitimately, to interpret and communicate the Gospel to an empirically-minded culture dominated by the natural sciences. Have they not made a too complete surrender to that with which they are trying to communicate and allowed an empiricist philosophy to dictate the terms of the debate, tailoring a supernatural faith to fit a naturalistic customer?

Believers have been caught with their clothes off by the theological explosion through ignorance of the philosophy behind it and the process of which it is the culmination — that steady erosion of metaphysics which has been going on since the Enlightenment. For a thousand years and more in the west the intellectual structure of Christian theism has been framed in a metaphysical scaffolding of a supporting and congenial philosophy. Under the impact of analytic philosophy that scaffolding has now collapsed, and some conclude that the house itself is in ruins.

In my view, Christian faith and experience necessitate belief in divine Transcendence. But merely to say that is not enough. I do not think that Christian theology will be healthy or confident or satisfying till we have succeeded in building up a new metaphysic or natural theology; and this, I believe, is most likely to emerge from an exploration of human personality which, while it has its roots in biochemistry, yet lives in a transcendent dimension. All this I tried to cram into a paperback called *Secular and Supernatural*, which has received some enthusiastic notices.

Thus, one way and another, the first seven years that I have spent on the episcopal shelf may not have been completely infertile.

I have lived through a period of immense change, more rapid and more revolutionary than any, probably, in recorded history, a period charged with crisis and upheaval, in which mankind is starting on a new era, the outcome of which nobody can predict. Today there is set before us life and death, unimagined new good or appalling evil, and the unanswered question of tomorrow is whether humanity has a future at all or will "perish through its own imaginations" and the dehumanisation of man. Both religiously and in every other way we live in a totally different society from that in which my generation grew up; if anyone who died in the pre-war world came back now, he would scarcely recognise it. Historians will no doubt mark off the last eighty years into two distinct periods; yet the period of my life has embraced both. What troubles me about what I have written is that though I have lived through momentous times, this has been largely a record of small and, as it may seem, trivial events, rather than of apocalyptic scenes, amid friends and colleagues who, though good and some great, were not of epic or world-changing stature. Can it have been, I ask myself, in any way a reflection or portrait of a period? Yet it is in fact through ordinary people doing day-by-day ordinary things, the immediate tasks and duties of the hour, in response to ever-changing situations — it is by such ways as this that history is made.

I shall not see the new age that is now being born. Yet when I consider the world in which we now are, it fills me, like Pilgrim, both with hope and fear. Our planet may yet be turned into a cemetery and the worship of gold may destroy the souls of men. There are few enough grounds for any secular optimism. A Christian is bound to be too well aware of the tragic dimension in human history to accept any facile predictions of infinite 'progress' through technology. And too many signs point in the other direction. We may be moving into the kind of world which the Bible associates with the reign of anti-Christ — dehumanised, cruel and catastrophic, in which the powers of evil seem victorious. The present civilisation may collapse and go down in a horror of anarchy and blood. There are certainly strong reasons for fear.

But there are stronger reasons for hope. I have hope for the future in which our grandchildren will grow up because I believe in God and the providential government of history. I believe that God raised Jesus from the dead and committed himself to the cause of Christ as his own cause. Good, yet undreamt of, is now within man's reach if we have the faith and courage to take it. Have we? What is paralysing men's wills today and driving them into the apathy of despair — of which the high suicide ratio in the most developed countries is one index — is the moral and spiritual vacuum at the heart of a secularised society, and the sheer lack of anything to believe in. England seems at the moment to be just drifting, undirected by any significant purpose, while the politicians have nothing to put before it beyond the primacy of material values. The irresponsible cult of permissiveness and the exploitation of sexuality are bringing us near the point of social breakdown; the reaction could be a dictatorship of the right, in which all liberal thinking is suppressed. But, as Mr. Quintin Hogg has observed recently — and almost alone among politicians he has had the courage to insist upon it — the only true path to ordered freedom is the recognition of absolute moral values; and the whole trend of opinion is against that. But has not the time come for the Church to say so? There are surely warnings enough in the Bible that if we forsake the Lord our God, we perish.

All over the world today men and women are seeking ways to break out from bondage and vindicate man's freedom and human dignity. Because of the frailty of our mortal nature some of these ways are false and some are dangerous. But who can doubt that the spirit of Christ is at work in them or that fundamentally this is a 'Christian' aim? Surely a prime part of the Church's mission is to work for the humanising of human life against all that threatens to dehumanise it, whether social, economic or intellectual? But we do not know what it is to be truly human if we leave out man's relation to God — which is what the Christian religion is about. Behind all the folly and the wickedness exploited by the media for money is the mass of ordinary 'decent' people, earning their livings and bringing up their families, trying to make of life something worthwhile and to find in it some satisfying meaning. The search for meaning is a religious quest. What guidance or leadership are they being offered?

In all the exercises in social criticism which appear in the press the Church is hardly ever so much as mentioned. It does not seem to have crossed the minds of editors that it would or could make any difference either way. What saddens me as I look on from the sidelines is that the Church seems to have so little to say. There is a powerful organised lobby working to extirpate Christianity from education and from the public philosophy. It is worrying that the Christian case is being too often allowed to go by default. The fundamental question before the Churches is not the modernising of their machinery, with which they are so introspectively preoccupied; it is whether Christianity is true. And the clergy themselves appear to be uncertain. It is one thing to be alive to the difficulties; a living faith will be always a questioning faith. We cannot meet men's problems and scepticisms by dishing out an unexamined traditionalism. But if the Churches give the impression of regarding the Gospel itself as an open question and the Being of God as an interesting hypothesis, how much moral authority can be left to them? People today do not greatly care about secondary questions of Church order, or the debates of ecclesiastical politics. They want to know what is right and what is wrong, who God is and how we can believe in him. I earnestly long to hear the Church again proclaiming a confident and positive faith, in a context of free thinking and honest criticism. That has been the humble attempt of my own ministry. Is it to be "never glad confident morning again"? Because I believe in God and the Resurrection, I do not accept that as the final word.

But just what is happening in the Church of England? It seems to be haunted by a disabling guilt, almost apologising for its existence. Some of its Bishops seem to feel the need to be always justifying their position, even to make public confessions that they ought not to be where they are at all. Self-criticism up to a point is salutary; but surely not to the point of abdication; and at times it seems now not to be very far from that.

We could see it beginning to happen at Toronto. It became apparent in one speech after another by Asian and African representatives how deep was the suspicion and even hatred of the ancient mother, the Church of England, and how little the respect for its achievements. No doubt it was part of the anti-colonial syndrome, and it was easy enough to make allowances; but it seems to have introduced a virus which has had a very debilitating effect on the thought not only of the Church of England but of the whole Anglican communion. Signs of a new and ultra-defensive attitude became clearly visible in the report of the 1968 Lambeth Conference. As *Theology* pointed out in an editorial that December:

The Servant Church—once a theological notion—is now becoming a serf church, in which Bishops are begrudged their titles (Resolution 41) and in which we 'cannot rightly speak of an inferior office' (Resolution 94). (Did the Bishops never recite *Quicunque vult*?) Service is in fact fully compatible with hierarchy: it is indeed an attribute of dignity—the supreme privilege of the highest is to serve. Service is incompatible with servitude. And this report (Lambeth 1968) most accurately reflects, instead of challenging, the paradox of the present mood, in which preoccupation with the miseries of the world, and anxiety for the Church to serve it, together result in too ready an acceptance of prescriptions which will reduce the Church to such servitude—to such sheer cultural poverty and social insignificance—that it becomes incapable of serving the world and doubtful of its own intrinsic worth.

"Doubtful of its own intrinsic worth"; and that does seem to describe the present mood, when prominent spokesmen repeatedly announce that the only useful function left for our Church and the Anglican communion is now to die. Even some of the rank and file of the clergy seem to have been seized by a strange, compulsive death-wish, as though one were watching, in some feverish nightmare, a suicide march of ecclesiastical lemmings. It is not for me just to sit here and criticise. But the Church does appear to be somehow losing its nerve; and I find all this perplexing in the extreme.

I may be one of the few survivors left who really do believe in the Church of England—not in 'anglicanism' but in this Church of England, as it has taken shape in this island with a thousand years of history behind it; and I cannot believe that the way to revitalise it is to try to turn into something different. But I cannot doubt that this would be the effect of some of the changes now being canvassed in one of the latest reports on the future of our Ministry. More than once I have stated my conviction, derived from a good many years of working experience, that the strength of our Church and the secret of its influence is the parish priest's responsible independence. Once you have undermined the parochial system and the Ministry by which it is now served and turned it into a streamlined bureaucracy, you will have gone far towards killing the Church of England. The proposed new deal is, in effect, a plan to alter the position of the Ministry from one of status to one of contract — just at the time when, in other walks of life, the defects of that process are being found out, and everyone is trying to go back on it, and work his way to an acknowledged status.

Under these proposals parish clergy would be deprived of their benefice freehold tenure to become ecclesiastical civil servants deployed by a central bureaucracy, if not employees of a corporation. All rights of patronage would be abolished and all appointments would henceforth be vested in an all-powerful diocesan committee, under a super-committee at Westminster. (It is odd that the smaller the membership of the Church, the more some people itch to increase the size and complexity, and incidentally the already enormous cost, of its organisation.) This would change the whole character of the Church of England, and it would, in my view, disastrously weaken the standing and influence of the parish priest. It is in right of his status as rector, as the man who is there to discharge that function, as the rector *of*, not a clergyman *in* a place, irremovable except by his own will, that he is given his pastoral opportunity.

It is, in my view, morally wrong to spend more on expensive administrative gadgets till the clergy have better pay and better pensions. The one really essential 'reform' is to get more and better qualified men into pastoral work, pay them properly, care for them and trust them.

But it is not only the parish priest whose independence would be eroded under this new deal, it is still more the bishop. And particularly in the matter of appointments. The question here is not merely that of finding a parish for a man who needs one, it is that of finding the right man for this parish; and here there is no substitute for the bishop. It would be a very bad thing for the Church if the bishop made all appointments directly, but from

none can he disinterest himself. (If a mistake is made, it is he
who must live with it, and he is the last man in the whole
Church who is likely to take appointments irresponsibly.) He
alone knows, or should know, as chief pastor, the particular
circumstances of the parish and also those personal or domestic
facts about the man under consideration which cannot, or
should not be, known to anyone else — least of all to an impersonal committee. Almost invariably he is consulted and in
practice it is he who has the last word. I should find it easier to
believe in the infallibility of bishops — heavily though it would
strain my credulity — than in the all-wisdom of a committee,
which would, in practice, function through an executive at
which the bishop would probably not be present, if not, in the
end, through a salaried lay secretary. The bishop would be
reduced to little more than a rubber stamp for its decisions. He
could not even license a curate or decide to what parish to send
him, unless the committee gave him permission. What kind of
man of what kind of quality would accept episcopal office on
such terms?

It is no part of the story of my life to examine these proposals,
or any others which have come up since I retired from office —
except to say this, that everything I have learnt in the course of
my ministry in the Church of England would lead me to resist
them, if I had to vote, not on grounds of octogenarian con-
servatism, but because I should not wish to vote for a death-
sentence. They would tear the Church up from its historical
roots to be replaced by a different society designed on the model
of industrial management. (Is that commonly thought to be
working all that well?) As William Temple discovered when he
was at Repton, "You cannot turn an old institution in a wholly
new direction and expect to be able to utilise its running powers
as before."[2]

All my life I have been a rebel against the Prayer Book and
clamouring for liturgical reform. I have had a hand in a number

[2] Iremonger's *Life*, p. 148.

of experiments. It amuses me that we now find ourselves looking around for churches in which we may still be vouchsafed the Liturgy of 1662. Many new proposals are now before the Church, issued by the Liturgical Commission. I have had no direct experience of any of them in actual use, except of the Communion office commonly known now as Series Two, at which I have not infrequently been present and have two or three times managed to celebrate. It may be a good service of Holy Communion, but how far is it the Eucharist of the Church? It seems to go very well in a school chapel or a village church or on a housing estate; in the Abbey it seems altogether out of place. No doubt there is too much upping and downing, which makes concentration of mind difficult; but that only calls for some minor rearrangement. My fundamental criticism would be that it tends to eliminate the transcendent mystery, the sense of a gift of grace coming out of the heart of things, a Beyond to which we are being always called.

In this, of course, it reflects a tendency common to all forms of the 'new' theology — and apparent in the New English Bible — of masking the ultimate mystery of God's being, which is surely what all religion is about. What an acceptable liturgy has to do is not merely to provide folksy worship but also to dramatise true theology. And I think no tentative forms could become permanent if they do not express the Otherness, the Transcendence, of That which is mediated through Christ, which is indispensable to Christianity. If we try to reduce our faith to common sense, to terms which are immediately thinkable, we shall only too easily succeed in killing it.

The other defect in the proposed new form is the poverty and weakness of its prose rhythms. These prayers can never be memorised, or become, like the rolling phrases of Cranmer's genius, part of the furniture of the minds of churchmen; and a great deal is going to be lost by that. Nor can the priest lead the worship of the people if he has to be reading something out of a book. He must have the services perfectly by heart. That is quite easy with 1662 — I have not used a Prayer Book for years.

Will it ever be possible with Series Two? This point, I suggest, is not finicky or captious; it concerns the whole psychology of worship and the function of the priest in liturgical leadership.

I have had to travel a long theological journey, on a continuous, ever-renewed quest. Neither for the Church nor the individual Christian is there any 'final' theology in this world, and while life lasts I hope to continue to learn. My intellectual interpretation and formulation of Christian belief has moved far from that of my early training — which is only to say that I did not stop growing. My parents and first teachers would be horrified if they knew what my theological views are now. (The theology of my ordinands at Southwell used to seem to me oddly old-fashioned and conventional — I was thinking far more radically than they were.) Yet in the end I have managed to combine a fairly advanced or liberal theology with an old-fashioned personal religion. I could not say, as William Temple said, that I have never known what it is to doubt the reality of God. Faith has had many an hour of doubt and darkness; but the darkness has not overcome it. What supports the individual pilgrim is the faith and experience of the Church; and within the Church I hold to the Christian faith. I believe in God and in man through Jesus Christ. The foundation of that faith is not in ideas, which must change with the changing movements of secular thought, but in the historical and living Person, yesterday and today the same and forever. Other foundation no man can lay. Apart from that Person the Church has no existence, and it seems to me, despite various criticisms, that its faith must always be massively Christo-centric. What we today call Christianity may undergo changes that we cannot envisage. What does not change is the irreducible Christ.

But the implications of that disclosure through that one historically conditioned Life are infinite and inexhaustible, and each generation ought to find new meanings in it. New meanings are being revealed today, some of which might have surprised or shocked our predecessors. But it is the same Christ and the same faith, even though, as well may be, with a changed emphasis in a changed human situation; and still the key to the human situation.

But it looks as though, in future, theology, if it is to interpret that faith to the world and interpret the world to itself by that faith, will have to work by rather different methods — not as an arcane, self-contained discipline but in inter-disciplinary dialogue; and indeed there are welcome signs that this is happening. To the twentieth century question, What is man? there can be neither a purely 'religious' nor a purely 'scientific' answer. Biochemistry and neurophysiology can tell us much about the human make-up which cannot be learnt from the Bible or 'Christian' sources, but must take their place in a Christian anthropology. Christian faith and experience can tell us what scientists, *qua* scientists, cannot know. If the Christian contribution is written off, then vastly important evidence is ignored. What light does the given fact of Jesus Christ throw on the total sum of available evidence? For, as D. M. Mackinnon has somewhere insisted, the Gospels record events and experiences which go beyond any 'ordinary' experience (and might fairly be described as meta-empirical) within a fragment of ordinary history — and this surely has a direct and decisive bearing on the positivist philosophy of this age and the current distrust of metaphysics.

I believe in God through the Man. Therefore I am able to believe in man, and, under God, in a future for man, and the victory of good over evil. And though the Church may seem now to be in decline — *all* institutions seem now to be in decline — yet, because I am able to hold to the Easter faith, I believe it will rise again in power and glory.

I have been allowed to enjoy a long life and have been preserved through many perils. Though to many it may sound narrow and unadventurous, it has yet been full, active and satisfying, enriched by many creative opportunities and supported by almost innumerable friendships. As I look back on it

I recall with thankfulness the hand of God's providence, leading me on from one stage to another, pulling me back from many false steps, strengthening me for new and difficult tasks, giving me blessings beyond all my deserving. No man can come so near the end of the day, after fifty-six years in Holy Orders, without being dreadfully aware of sins and negligences, defeats and failures, evil committed and good left undone. Thanksgiving must be expressed in penitence.

But I would have my last word to be one of gratitude — for such gifts as may have been entrusted to me, for the many friends in all walks of life in all parts of the world, who have stood by me and strengthened me by their encouragement and example — and to few of these do we owe deeper gratitude than to the company of beloved physicians who have ministered to our souls and bodies — for my parents who bore me and gave me my religion, for the education which nourished my growing mind, for the colleagues who have worked with me so generously; for our forty years of devoted marriage, crowned by seeing our daughter happily married, with clever children round about their table; and chiefly for her who has been my life's partner, to whom I owe most of what is best in me. For these and all other blessings I give thanks to the Lord of Life and the Giver of all good.

My title virtually dictates the epilogue:

> Through ev'ry period of my life
> Thy goodness I'll pursue,
> And after death in distant worlds
> The glorious theme renew.

> Through all eternity to thee
> A joyful song I'll raise;
> But Oh, eternity's too short
> To utter all thy praise.

Postscript

THERE THE BOOK in its original form ended. Since then, however, and while it was being printed, our family has again been stricken by a sudden, overwhelming tragedy which has left Rosemary desolate for the second time; and I cannot let the proofs go without some mention of it. My first thought was to redraft the final paragraph, for had I been writing that page today it could not be in quite the same words. I decided, however, to leave it just as it stands. For if, as is probable, this is my last book, that is what I should wish to be my last word. This blow has come to us as a numbing shock, and we grieve not least for the young children. But we must not allow the sorrow that has fallen on us to detract from our thankfulness to God for the happiness given to us in the past, or obscure the faith by which we have tried to live.

Old men have long 'kept watch on man's mortality'. For fifty years and more I have tried to minister to people in pain, bereavement or despair. What should be said to them? What can be said to them? For glib 'religious' phrases can mean little. When these things happen, most men and women in their distress and bewilderment cry out Why? Why has God inflicted this cruel hurt on us? To that question, I think, there may be no answer within the reach of the finite understanding. We are creatures; we did not make or design the world; and we cannot know why it is the way it is. Man's life and death are surrounded by mystery, and of that mystery suffering is one element. I should want to say that God does not 'send' it, in the sense that God does not intervene directly in the nexus of physical causation. But to say that does not answer the question.

Why? Jesus himself does not seem to have known the answer. But in agony in the Garden he accepted it, and taught men how to suffer and overcome. Through it he revealed God victorious, and his cross became the symbol of Christian faith. I do not think there is any possibility, in this actual, tragic world we know, of believing in God who is a God of love, except through Christ crucified and risen.

But a last-minute addition is no place for the exploration of theological depths — it was meant as no more than a note to a personal record. What I am most anxious to do here is to offer humble and grateful recognition of the wonderful way in which people have stood by us, in a benediction of support and friendship which has been for us a light shining in darkness. Men and women in all walks of life have spared nothing to bring us help and kindness. Old and trusted friends the world over have upheld us by prayers, words and deeds. And the almost unbelievable generosity of the gift from the parishioners of Westbourne (of which our son-in-law was the Rector) is something that none of us can ever forget. This volume of spontaneous love beyond all our deserts has brought us strength and healing, and has been to me a fresh revelation of redemptive Love at the ultimate heart of things. I feel constrained to say — for it may help others — that this ministry of human succour has enabled us to go on believing in God, the Father of our Lord Jesus Christ.

Table of Dates

List of Main Publications

The Relevance of Christianity (Nisbet)
The Relevance of the Church (Nisbet)
What Has Christianity to Say? (SCM)
I Heard a Voice (Christophers)
Faith in Dark Ages (SCM)
Church and Leadership (SCM)
The Recovery of Man (Nisbet)
Vocation and Ministry (Nisbet)
Asking the Right Questions (Hodder and Stoughton)
Mervyn Haigh (SPCK)
Questioning Faith (SCM Paperbacks)
Christian Ethics and Secular Society (Hodder and Stoughton)
Weep Not For Me (Pergamon Press)
The Atonement (Hodder and Stoughton)
Secular and Supernatural (SCM Paperbacks)
Period of My Life (Hodder and Stoughton)

Index